In the beginning God created the heaven and the earth.

And the earth was without form, and void; and darkness *was* upon the face of the deep. And the Spirit of God moved upon the face of the waters.

And God said, Let there be light: and there was light.

And God saw the light, that *it was* good: and God divided the light from the darkness.

And God called the light Day, and the darkness he called Night.

And God saw every thing that he had made, and, behold, *it was* very good. And the evening and the morning were the sixth day.

Thus the heavens and the earth were finished, and all the host of them.

And on the seventh day God ended his work which he had made; and he rested on the seventh day from all his work which he had made. . . .

# ...THAT WAS THE WEEK THAT WAS

# THAT WAS THE WEEK THAT WAS

### EDITED BY

## David Frost & Ned Sherrin

W. H. ALLEN
LONDON
1963

This is a miscellany of material from a new television programme called
That Was The Week That Was.

We would like to thank the writers who wrote it.

We would like to thank the performers whose work on it was a
combination of interpretation, transformation and mutilation. This
book records what happened when they got together. . . .

D. F. & N. S.

*Printed and bound in Great Britain by William Clowes and Sons, Ltd.*
*London and Beccles, for the publishers W. H. Allen & Co., Essex Street, London W.C.2*

# Contents

To Timothy Birdsall

# 1 Show Business

## A Parable    Peter Veale

A SON SAT at the knee of his father, and uttered a word that was forbidden. His father, being a righteous man, chastised him.

In the fullness of time, the boy became a man and asked a maiden's hand in marriage, but the maiden scorned him, for he was wont to utter the word that was forbidden, and she thought it not nice.

So the young man sought counsel of his elders, and betook himself to a place of entertainment, where so many resorted that were wise in the ways of the world, and there he uttered the forbidden word many times nightly, and all laughed.

The multitude said: That which was dark is now light, and we have the freedom of the word that was forbidden. And the father of the young man cherished him, and the comely maiden married him, after that he had promised he would utter the forbidden word only in a place of entertainment, for a reward of gold.

Verily it is said, a word is judged not by the number of its letters, but by the company it keeps.

## WHAT IS A NORTHERNER?    Keith Waterhouse & Willis Hall

A NORTHERNER IS a scrap of humanity moulded by God in his own image, swathed in a cloth cap and set down in the Metropolis to love and be loved by Oscar Lewenstein, Nat Cohen, Stuart Levy, Sidney Bernstein and, until quite recently, Kenneth Tynan and Harold Hobson.

Others were born with silver spoons in their mouths but the Northerner was born with a silver shovel in his.

Life has been good to the Northerner.

He had nothing to say and they called him dour.

He had a vocabulary of 450 words and they praised his plain speaking.

He was rude, coarse and pig-ignorant and they called him blunt.

The Northerner is a dreamer and a maker of films. He introduced Lancashire to the Americans, who thought it was Yorkshire, and to Penelope Gilliatt, who thought it was the Midlands. He showed the world that beneath their simple cotton frocks even mill girls are stark staring naked.

The Northerner is a dramatist. He abolished insipid dialogue such as 'Anyone for tennis?' and replaced it with biting, incisive lines such as 'Would you like a cup of tea?' He captured everyday turns of speech that no one even knew had escaped.

The Northerner is an actor. He appeared in slice-of-life dramas and then for fear of being typecast played Hamlet—with a northern accent.

The Northerner is a sociologist. He described in minute detail the working life of a northern street—and then condemned the television system that does exactly the same thing in 'Coronation Street' twice a week.

The Northerner is the Messiah of television and his message is that everybody north of the River Trent is ordinary folk. Ordinary criminals shoot ordinary bank managers and are arrested by ordinary policemen. That is how life is lived.

The Northerner is a novelist. He has drawn on the rich heritage of the broad acres and with the blood and bitterness of Peterloo, the Wars of the Roses and the Industrial Revolution behind him he has produced a best-seller showing exactly what happens when a shop-girl gets put in the family way.

The Northerner is a thinker and a philosopher. He has passed off platitudes as epigrams with a wave of the pipe and the words 'Let's get down to brass tacks'.

Beneath every Northern watch-chain is a Southerner screaming to be let out. That is why the Northerner has come South—but he has not lost his simplicity. He still prefers the simple foods of his boyhood. He eats fish and chips at the Caprice, bacon and eggs at the Ivy and on one democratic evening he ordered a pork pie at the Savoy Grill. He may own a Bentley but he always sits with the chauffeur.

The Northerner has two dreams. The first dream is of the pit heaps he knew as a child— only in his dreams they are heaps of money. The second dream is a nightmare and goes as follows: What would have happened to him—what in God's name would have happened— if he'd had the gross misfortune to have been born in Maidenhead?

## WHAT IS A LOVEABLECOCKNEYSPARRER?

Keith Waterhouse & Willis Hall

A LOVEABLECOCKNEYSPARRER IS one whose theory it is that maybe it's because he's a Londoner that he loves London so—a form a narcissism encountered nowhere else in the British Isles.

The true loveablecockneysparrer was born within the sound of Bow Bells, but the even truer loveablecockneysparrer was born within the sound of the Blitz. This was a series of aerial bombardments twenty years ago and it forms the basis of all loveablecockneyfolklore, which is collated from time to time in the London *Evening News* under the heading 'More Readers' Bomb Stories'.

Apart from bomb stories the loveablecockneysparrer has no real culture. London Pride has been handed down to him but it was handed down to him by Charles Dickens, who came from Portsmouth, and by Noel Coward, who was born in Teddington. The loveablecockneymuse is now celebrated by loveablecockneycomposers who cannot read music and by loveablecockneyauthors, most of them lately out of prison, who cannot write English.

The loveablecockneysparrer has, himself, however, an enviable command of the English tongue. He uses language which elsewhere would be deemed obscene but which in Billingsgate is described as colourful. He has a touch of the poet and rhymes 'stairs' with 'apples and pears'. He is a wit in his own right and is famous for his repartee. This consists almost entirely of leaning out of cab windows and hailing passing bubble cars with the *mot*: 'What you got there, guv, a goldfish bowl?'. These sayings are collected by the London *Evening News* under the heading 'More Cockney Humour'.

A wit himself, the loveablecockneysparrer appreciates wit in others. During the loveablecockneyblitz the epigram 'Can I do yer now, sir?', with its spicy double entendre, so appealed to him that, like Oscar Wilde after Whistler, he was tempted to pass it off as his own.

The loveablecockneysparrer loves mums, grans, kids, tea, royalty, eels, whelks, 'Appy 'Amstead, and most of all his own witty, wiry, cheeky, chirpy, irrepressible self. His motto is 'London can take it', and as he dons his pearly suit, prepares for yet another round of 'Knees Up Mother Brown' and drags us kicking and screaming back into the nineteenth century, perhaps we can be forgiven for remarking that London can keep it.

When you pass the London Palladium, think how many great entertainers have struggled to rise in their profession.

Consider Stubby DeLuxe Junior —Mister Marvellous himself.

As a small boy in Jamaica, Stubby DeLuxe would often lead the calypsos on his hand trumpet.

*Day-o, day-dayay-o.*

On ceremonial occasions, such as royal visits, Stubby would use the formidable two-handed trumpet.

One day Stubby said: 'Man, I feel, I'm ready for de Palladium . . . wow!'

He arrived in London, capital of the Commonwealth, with his lucky leopard-skin coat and juju stick.

He quickly made friends with some social workers, who told him where he might find a bed.

*STUBBY'S PROGRESS*       Written by Leslie Mallory & Lewis Morley

But he already had an address his married sister had given him.

However, although Stubby was ready for the Palladium, the Palladium was not ready for him.

'It can't be my skin. Look at all those coloured LP's in the shops.'

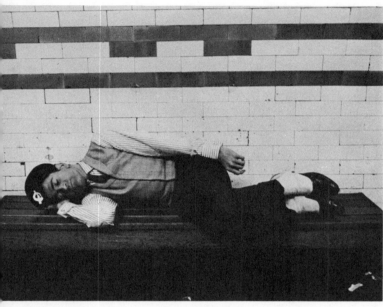

So Stubby accepted a position with London Transport, where he composed and performed his most famous blues.

'Mind the Doors.'

The passengers liked it, but London Transport thought it rather advanced.

One day Stubby forgot and used the dreaded two-handed trumpet. 'All Change!'

Stubby was sent back to the surface.

But working in the Underground had weakened his eyesight, so he had to put on his shades.

A kindly theatrical agent thought he was blind and helped him across the street.

He launched Stubby on a new business career. Refusing to accept more than 75 per cent. 'Day-O!'

He met a progressive young actress who got him into the C.N.D.

Which Stubby innocently thought stood for Colour No Drawback.

His records were selling. He was able to buy a charming little town house.

At last came the great night.

Stubby appeared in the Royal Variety Performance.

From the stage of the London Palladium he led the audience in the homely, comforting words of the National Anthem.

And so we leave him there in his moment of triumph, a gifted son of the Commonwealth who has proved once again what all of us know. . . . . .

**New, Exciting Britain—**

**Best for Whites and Coloureds too.**

## MARILYN

*Dedicated to Christopher Hassall*

*In the first week of 1963 Madame Tussaud's melted down the wax figures of a number of men and women who had fallen from public fame a little. They included Marilyn Monroe, Vivien Leigh, Lord Kilmuir, Marshal Voroshilov, Lt.-Col. Harry Llewellyn, Selwyn Lloyd and Terry Spinks. Their wax went towards a new model of James Hanratty, the A6 murderer.*

Flames whisper now their threnody
O'er Voroshilov and Vivien Leigh;
Flames disrespectful, not for quelling
Melt Lord Kilmuir and Col. Llewellyn;
And the consuming flames now shrinks
The waxwork form of Terry Spinks;
Flames are the cradle, flames the lace
That frame sweet Marilyn's radiant face.

Ashes to ashes,
Wax to flame;
Selwyn and Marilyn the same.

Furnaceman, as you stir the pot,
Ponder a moment on this lot—
Brave travellers on Fame's golden tracks
Reduced, now to amorphous wax.
Beauty, brains, brawn and personal symmetry
Boiled in your cauldron to anonymity,
The cheaper to achieve the morrow's
Attraction in the Chamber of Horrors.

Ashes to ashes,
Wax to flame;
Selwyn and Terry Spinks the same.
Spare, friend, a sigh for Vivien there,
But for sweet Marilyn a prayer.

## LAY WASTE THE LILIES

*Through the early months of 1963 a rumour, busy and persistent, was going the rounds that permission had been sought to build a block of skyscrapers in the lake-side garden of Anna Pavlova's house in London, on the edge of Golders Hill Park—Pavlova, the for-all-time ballerina, who eloquently danced to limpid music 'The Dying Swan'.*

Must they lay waste the lilies?
Where once Pavlova's swans went swanning by
Set up their glass-walled tower in the sky;
Uproot Pavlova's garden? Banish the black-
 bird—
From Golders Hill to Greenwich none is heard.
Fill in the lake where sunning swan could preen
To the attentive dancer on the green.
Obliterate, now that her swan-song's done,
The Ballerina, pausing in the sun.

City-builders, who dream crystal and steel,
Dream high, build high, sail high,
And snatch a new dimension from the sky,
And London has sprouted a thin forest of
 glass—
Stiff cubic trees; hutches for humans.
But what can a hutch say to the heart? Re-
 iterate
A steep steel right to dominate,
Where on a lawn that's gone
Pavlova, in a green world, watched a swan.

**Both poems by Caryl Brahms**

JOCASTA'S SONG

*Early one morning*
*Just as my son was rising . . .*

# SUBTITLES *or* WHAT SPORTING LIFE?　Derek Lowe

THE NEW WAVE in British cinema, wallowing under the kitchen sink, has revealed an apparent contradiction in terms, for it seems that as these films grow more and more outspoken (i.e. profitable) so the protagonists become almost completely inarticulate. A recent example of this was the frank Rugby Football Love Story of Frank and his widow landlady. Frank, you may recall, had difficulty getting into touch with the widow landlady. This classic film of a Scrum Half's passion, with its mumbled skeletal dialogue and dramatic pauses, cried out for English Subtitles; these would have helped more imperceptive members of the audience to realise just what was being implied.

WIDOW: *That you, Frank?*
SUBTITLE: Withdrawn from life, I sit here, drooping over the memory of my late husband, watching 'Compact', cut off from all emotion until this great ape comes blundering in.

FRANK: *Yes, it's me.*
SUBTITLE: Me, the rough and uncouth, savage, tragic scrum half, big built, muscular and self-sufficient with it.

WIDOW: *How did the match go?*
SUBTITLE: As if I had any real interest the brutal, gladiatorial spectacle of the over-grown schoolboys, racing, tacklin cannonading about some muddy pitc

FRANK: *We won.*
SUBTITLE: I can't wait to get you into bed, you bundle of sensuality, and attempt once more to batter down your reserve, hoping beyond hope that you might say, when I have done, that you enjoyed it.

WIDOW: *What happened to you?*
SUBTITLE: Not that I greatly care, sitting here semi-detached from life, locked in memory's lavatory, remembering other happier days.

FRANK: *Nothing much.*
SUBTITLE: During a scrum in the seco half, some rotten bastard of a half-ba put his big boot into my panting mou knocking out all my front teeth, leav behind bloody stumps and bleed gums.

IDOW: *Does it hurt?*
BTITLE: His face looks an absolute mess, what will the neighbours think?

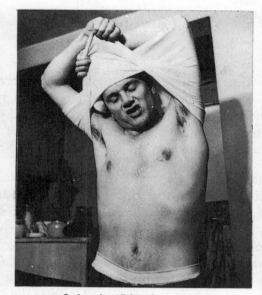

FRANK: *Only when I laugh.*
SUBTITLE: And there is nothing to laugh at in this futile ridiculous life. Nothing. I mean nothing to her and she means nothing to me, I keep telling myself.

WIDOW: *I'll mash a pot of tea.*
SUBTITLE: It is difficult to make a decision in the present when your mind is forever in the past, but I had better make the effort and tell him, now, this minute.

RANK: *Yes. You do that.*
BTITLE: She is acting funny tonight, as though she has some dark thought on her mind that she must spew up into words in order to obtain relief. However, I shall tell her my good news and hope for some reaction.

FRANK: *I've turned Pro, you know——*

WIDOW: *Have you, well, I've got news for you. So have I. Next time you want it, you can pay for it.*

# RADIO ARMENIA    Caryl Brahms

A COPY OF Czechoslovakia's first satirical newspaper arrived in Britain recently. *Nase Pravo*—'Our Justice'—is produced secretly and delivered regularly by post every other week to every telephone subscriber in Prague. If discovered the editors would certainly be charged with treason and espionage. In Russia this sort of thing has flourished in a less organised way for some time—for example:

The Director of Radio Armenia went off on a visit to Moscow. Before leaving he arranged to write to his friends in blue ink if he found conditions easier there, and in red ink if things were bad. So off he goes to Moscow and he sends his letter home and it's written in blue ink and it says: 'Everything is fine here in Moscow—only I haven't been able to find any red ink!'

Every satirical remark is attributed to the non-existent Radio Armenia—the laughter is secret, grim and down to earth. It is applied laughter—laughter applied to the diminishment of terror by ridicule. And before 'applying' it you take a good look over your shoulder.

'My radio tells me there is plenty of food in the shops, but my refrigerator is empty. What do I do?'
'Put your radio into your refrigerator.'

'Could Communism be established in Sweden?'
'Yes, but it would be an awful pity.'

'An Armenian schoolboy wrote an essay about three new-born kittens. They were round, fluffy and two were communists.'
'Why only two?'
'Well, the third one opened its eyes yesterday.'

'They said on Radio Armenia today that Adam and Eve were Russians—can this be proved?'
'Sure! They were poor. They had nothing to wear. And they believed they were living in Paradise!'

Sometimes the message is domestic, like the day when the Director of Radio Armenia made a call on Major Gagarin.
'Major Gagarin is in orbit. He won't be back for an hour.'
'Can I speak to Mrs Gagarin, then?'
'She's buying meat—she won't be back for four hours!'

The change of Soviet official front over Stalin presented the Director of Radio Armenia with a golden vein of Armenian satire; and Radio Armenia dealt faithfully with the difficulty Khrushchev met with in the early stages of disposing of Stalin's displaced corpse. His offer to send Kennedy the exhibit in a glass coffin was turned down because of American customs duties. General de Gaulle said No because he feared it might set the Unknown Soldier turning in his grave. As for Macmillan, he'd got into quite enough trouble what with Karl Marx's monument already in London. Dr Adenauer, of course, deeply deprecated any supposition that a head of state could be mortal. Finally Nikita was forced to appeal to Ben Gurion who cabled back a reply from Egypt. 'Offer accepted stop. Must, however, warn you. We in Israel have already had unfortunate repercussions from an earlier resurrection.'

The Director of Radio Armenia was tremendously impressed by the production chart on the wall of a soviet factory.

'5,000 the first year, 50,000 the next, 500,000 this year, you'll be up to a million soon, what do you make?'

'Out-of-order notices.'

The last story from Radio Armenia has a ring of finality about it.

'Have you heard? The Director of Radio Armenia has committed suicide.'

'No! Why?'

'Well, he read on the front page of *Pravda* that Russia was overtaking America, and he turned to the middle page and read that America is standing at the edge of an abyss and . . .'

# USE **FILTH** LIKE MRS M. M. OF WEMBLEY PARK

**BEFORE**

**AFTER**

# Only 1/6 a time — or two for 3/-

**Wait a minute, though. . . .**

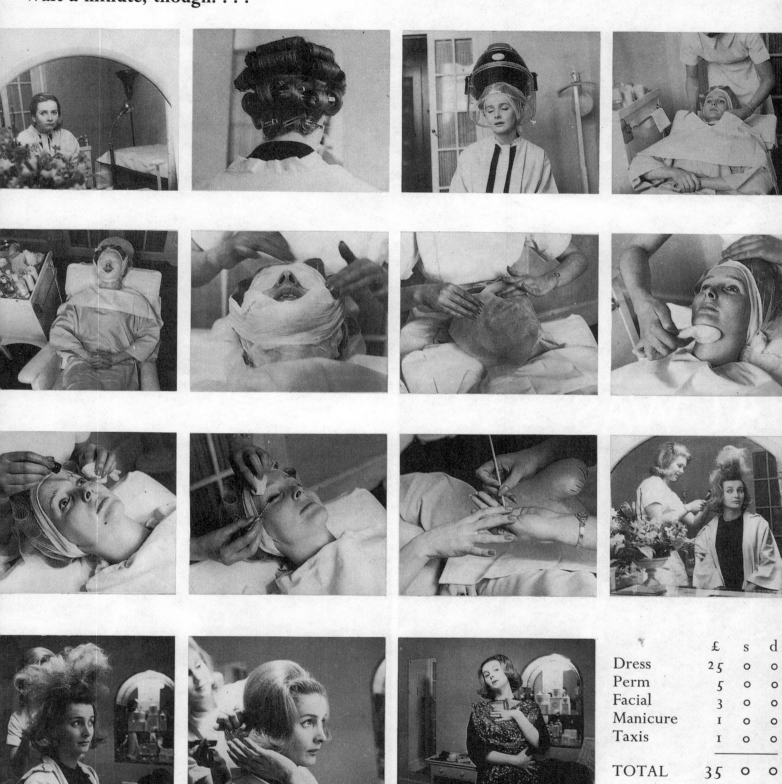

| | £ | s | d |
|---|---|---|---|
| Dress | 25 | o | o |
| Perm | 5 | o | o |
| Facial | 3 | o | o |
| Manicure | 1 | o | o |
| Taxis | 1 | o | o |
| TOTAL | 35 | o | o |

**Mind you, they didn't bother with any FILTH, so that did save 1/6.**

THAT WAS THE WEEK THAT WAS

KEEP THE BOMB

PHOTOGRAPHS BY
JOHN TIMBERS

# 2 Politics

*MACHIAVELLI*      Peter Lewis & Peter Dobereiner

'I think Harold's sincere, don't you?'

'No doubt of it. And, you know, I believe Wilson's sincere, too.'

'And you've only got to look at Jo to see that he's sincere.'

'Utterly. For that matter, there's no questioning that Jack Kennedy's sincere.'

'Oh yes. Come to that, so's Khrushchev. Give him his due, whatever else he may be, he's sincere.'

'True, true. Thank God there aren't any Machiavellis in world politics today.'

'You knew where you were with Machiavelli.'

*Aren't there a lot more black people than white ones in South Africa, and so shouldn't they perhaps run the country?*

Of course there are, that is precisely the point. There are so many more of them they have less need to say as much as the few white people.

*Yes, I see. How very silly of me. But even so wouldn't they like a chance?*

There you go again, with your old European ideals. In a new civilisation like ours we can't leave things to *chance*.

*Of course not. But it seems to some people that you leave very little to chance, what with house arrest and barbed wire round the native villages.*

This is just the kind of thing our critics are always raising. Dear me! In Africa, you see, words like house have quite a different meaning. Until recently the Bantus didn't even have houses, never knew the word. So, as you can imagine, house arrest gives people a sort of prestige—a status symbol. And you mentioned barbed wire around villages. That's just the sort of distortion which journalists are always putting about. I can imagine a Bantu coming to London and thinking all houses with railings in front of them were prisons. Ha ha! If, of course, the Bantus were allowed to come to London. . . .

*I am so glad you have cleared that up for me. You don't think then that black people are inferior to white people?*

Of course not. If we did do you think we'd go to all this trouble to suppress them?

Quentin Crewe

# 'ADMIRALTY FOR SALE'    Peter Lewis & Peter Dobereiner

MR THORNEYCROFT ANNOUNCED early in the year that the Admiralty, the War Office and the Air Ministry were to be merged, with their ministers, into a single Ministry of Defence housed in one building. Whether or not this makes our defence any cheaper, it's bound to mean that there will be some spare accommodation going in Whitehall. What a chance for that poet of the Sunday paper property columns, Mr Roy Brooks.

Unfashionable Whitehall. Superfluous First Lord, joining ranks of unemployed, forced to sacrifice hideous town residence built 1726 in the days when admirals had work to do.

Squalid and inconvenient interior compensated by interesting historical associations with Pepys, Blake, Barham, Nelson, Fisher and, coming to our own times, Vassall.

Board room contains wind compass of 1710 operated by vane on roof, probably unreliable as present occupant had no idea which way wind was blowing.

Also adjoining outbuildings known as Admiralty House occupied by quiet statutory tenant (old-age pensioner). You would not honestly know he was there. Vacant possession can be expected at next General Election. *View Sunday*. **TRY ANY OFFER.**

## DEFENCE    John Albery

1963 IS NOT the first year in which this country has had a Defence Policy. Six years ago, Harold Macmillan became Prime Minister, and Mr Antony Head lost his, and in his place at the Ministry of Defence reigned Mr Duncan Sandys, who is, of course, a son-in-law of Sir Winston Churchill. By April of the same year, with the Prime Minister's blessing, he had produced a White Paper which in its own words:

'. . . sets out the biggest change in military policy ever made in normal times.' (WHITE PAPER CI24, P. 9, SECTION 67.)

This was the White Paper which put its trust in a policy of big bangs and small forces. Here was enshrined the mystical doctrine of the Independent British Deterrent. Here was a policy which above all meant the end of conscription. Regiments were amalgamated; senior officers scrapped, and divisions melted into brigades. How else could the Government pay for a pre-election boom? On 25th February 1959 Mr Duncan Sandys spoke in the House of Commons.

'I am confident that our decision to continue with the development of Blue Streak is the right course and in fact that any other course would involve a wholly unprofitable gamble.'

And on the eve of Macmillan's pantomime visit to Moscow the *Evening News* proudly proclaimed:

'Blue Streak wins. Macmillan will talk from Strength.'

A new Cabinet and a new Minister of Defence: Mr Harold Watkinson, son-in-law to no one in particular. In February 1960 he produced his first White Paper.

'The development of the British ballistic missile Blue Streak is continuing. . . .'

On 8th February Mr Sandys, now busy 'reorganising' the aircraft industry out of existence, could say in the House:

'I know of no intention to discontinue the development of Blue Streak.' (HANSARD, 8TH FEBRUARY 1960, COL. 20.)

But eight weeks later, on 13th April, Mr Watkinson announced that Blue Streak would be cancelled.

'In the debate this year I was very careful to say that we had this question under examination. It is a right decision this year as it would have been a wrong decision last year.' (HANSARD, 13TH APRIL 1960, COL. 1269.)

But Mr James Callaghan was wondering . . .

'Where the Minister of Aviation is and when he is going to resign.'

Of course Mr Sandys had no intention of resigning. He told the House:

'If Blue Streak had been carried through to completion I am confident that it could have had as fine a performance as any medium-range rocket in Russia or America.' (HANSARD, 27TH APRIL 1960, COL. 331.)

Only it would have been five years too late. As Mr Harold Wilson said:

'He finds a goose, and tells us in one White Paper that it's a swan—until we have finished paying for it; then it's a dead duck.' (HANSARD, 27TH APRIL 1960, COL. 325.)

A Defence Policy based on Faith and Hope was now strengthened by the addition of Charity. The Americans agreed that we should be allowed to purchase Skybolt, and so we started what Mr Sandys himself had called only a year previously 'a wholly unprofitable gamble.'

Mr Watkinson, as usual, was confident:

'To say that Skybolt makes us dependent on the United States is as inaccurate as it would be to say that the welcome purchase of British motor cars by many Americans makes the United States dependent on us for transport.' (THE TIMES, 4TH JULY 1960.)

On April 27th a backbencher raised his voice in protest, Mr Antony Head:

'My real fear about Skybolt is that in five years' time, when the bill comes in, it will be more than was thought and that there will be other weapons coming along. That expenditure will have to be met at the expense of other defence commitments particularly our conventional forces.' (HANSARD, 27TH APRIL 1960.)

Ten weeks later he was kicked not only upstairs but outside, and from Lagos the embarrassing voice of Viscount Head can no longer be heard.

Not a drum was heard; not a funeral note, when, on 13th July 1962, Mr Watkinson was replaced by Mr Peter Thorneycroft. Mr Thorneycroft started in the traditional manner by cancelling a missile. On 11th August Blue Water and £25 million went west. But other people can also cancel missiles. On 13th December Skybolt was discontinued, for the best reasons: Mr Kennedy said . . .

'We have put $350 million into Skybolt. No other country has put anything into its actual manufacture.' (THE TIMES, 18TH DECEMBER 1962.)

In the House of Commons Mr Thorneycroft admitted:

'I am aware that there are men who believe passionately that we should strip this country of her deterrent.'

So, on 15th December Britain's ultimate weapon was launched: dangerous, expensive, obsolescent and lacking in credibility, it arrived in Nassau. It returned on Christmas Eve mumbling about independence and interdependence. Perhaps ultradependence would be a fairer description. For about £325 million the country would be able to buy Polaris submarines. But, of course,

'Britain was right to have looked to Skybolt, but equally right to change over now.' (THE TIMES, 24TH DECEMBER 1962, P. 8.)

On Wednesday, 2nd January, Mr Thorneycroft had to placate his fellow Conservative backbenchers by promising to fill the missile gap with a new stand-off bomb. This was of course to ensure that Mr Thorneycroft's successor would have a missile to cancel, too.

## LIBERAL HELPING     David Frost & Christopher Booker

*Meetings in Washington always sound pretty high-powered. Even, for instance, when Jo Grimond, with his seven seats in the House of Commons, confronted the President of the Western World, John F. Kennedy. But what on earth did they say to each other. . . .*

K: Well now, Lloyd George, how would government by your Party differ from the other two?

G: Well, basically, myself as Prime Minister, you see.

K: Certainly neither of the others would consider that. But what's your line in programs?

G: Well, we've been urging the Government to go into Europe for years.

K: It doesn't seem to have had much effect, does it?

G: No, that's what's so rotten actually. It's always happening to us. But *we* were urging them to go into Europe long before the Common Market was ever thought of.

K: But come on, Asquith, you don't spend all your time recalling things you've said in the past, do you?

G: Oh, yes. Yes, we do. You should hear some of the things we said in 1906, for instance. Like 'We've won!'

K: But I won in 1960.

G: Yes, well, so did I. Beccles Urban District Council elections. Liberal gain from Independent. What a night that was at our Victoria Street H.Q. The South African sherry flowing like water. Which it was, mainly.

K: One of your two minutes is gone, Mr Bonham Carter.

G: Yes, well we see ourselves as the sort of British New Frontiersmen. . . .

K: That's all very well, but I still don't see what the difference is between you and the Labour Party?

G: About 250 seats in the House of Commons.

# The Devlin Report: A Grimm Fairy Tale

## JOHN ALBERY & DAVID MASON

IN 1963 NYASALAND gained her independence and the telegrams flooded in to the new Prime Minister, Dr Hastings Banda.

Julius Nyerere said: 'Kwacha! Good wishes and congratulations!'

Mr Chester Bowles, President Kennedy's special adviser on African and Asian affairs, said: 'I recall with great satisfaction my rewarding talks with you last autumn. You have our warm support.'

And the First Secretary of State, Mr R. A. Butler, said: 'My own warmest sentiments to you personally. May I at the same time express the hope that we shall in years to come maintain the happy and cordial relationship between Nyasaland and the United Kingdom.'

Once upon a time, a long time ago, in 1959 to be exact, in the middle of darkest Nyasaland there lived an African. He was called Little Black Banda. Now Little Black Banda was frightfully clever, and he had lots and lots of friends. But he also had three enemies. There was the Welensky, who wanted to be an engine driver when he grew up, but he never did. There was the Lennox-Boyd, who ruled over the Colonies with an iron hand concealed in an iron glove. But worst of all his enemies there was the Governor, Sir Robert Armitage. He had been Governor of Cyprus when EOKA started, but that's another story.

One day Little Black Banda shouted at the Governor and the Governor became very frightened. 'They're planning to murder me', he told the Lennox-Boyd. 'They're planning to murder the Governor of Nyasaland', the Lennox-Boyd told Uncle Mac. 'Where?', asked Uncle Mac, who was used to this sort of thing from the Lennox-Boyd. 'Murder plot', screamed all the papers. 'Diabolical murder plot', screamed the Welensky. The Governor had by now worked himself up into a proper state of emergency and he decided to arrest Little Black Banda, and because he was very frightened he sent: a Search Group of two special branch men, an Escort Group of three special constables, a snatch party of six men under a police inspector, a diversion group of a police inspector and six men, a support group of a whole platoon of King's African Rifles and an Assault group of a whole platoon of PMF.

Poor Little Black Banda, when he had been searched, escorted, snatched, diverted, supported and assaulted, was taken to the airport in his dressing gown and put on an aeroplane for Southern Rhodesia, where the Welensky was waiting for him. But some of Little Black Banda's friends were less fortunate than this. Fifty-one of them were shot. Shoot back? They didn't have any guns. Some had their houses burnt; they were not even given time to remove their belongings. Now this was not exactly within the law, but the Provincial Commissioner said that he did it to ensure that 'looting, intimidation and arson were stamped out as quickly as possible'. What is arson, child? You may well ask. Within a month the Governor had detained about a thousand of Little Black Banda's friends. Detained, my dear? Imprisoned without trial.

**M**eanwhile, faraway in England some people were saying that the Governor and the Lennox-Boyd had blundered, and even that there was no murder plot. So Uncle Mac told the Lennox-Boyd to choose himself a Commission to prove that he was right, and the Lennox-Boyd chose Lord Justice Devlin, a Judge in the High Court; Sir John Ure Primrose, Chairman of Scottish Motor Traction Ltd.; Sir Percy Wynn Harris, Ex-Governor of Gambia; and Brigadier Williams, Warden of Rhodes House. And the Commission travelled all over Nyasaland and saw lots of people, and in July they published the truth in a little blue book.

**W**e have rejected the evidence, such as it is, for the murder plot', said the Devlin report. And again: 'Nyasaland is, no doubt only temporarily, a police state, where it is not safe for anyone to express approval of the policies of the Congress Party to which, before 3rd March, 1959, the vast majority of politically minded Africans belonged, and where it is unwise to express any but the most restrained criticism of Government policy.' The Lennox-Boyd was so upset that for a moment he offered to resign, but Uncle Mac said that would be pointless and ridiculous, because after all there was going to be an election in three months' time. So Uncle Mac and the Lennox-Boyd brought out the Manninghambuller, a machine they used at times to obscure really dangerous issues. And when they had wound him up he made his speech. And though he had never set foot in Nyasaland, all the Tory MP's believed him rather than Lord Justice Devlin. The voice of the Turton was heard in the land saying that if the Lennox-Boyd left his post, a light would be extinguished in the Commonwealth that would be extremely hard to rekindle. The Marquess of Salisbury preferred the harsher realities of administration to the legal niceties of the Law Courts, and Lord Coleraine attacked Lord Justice Devlin for his intellectual dishonesty and said that long after his report was pigeon-holed it would continue to poison relations between black and white. And so the Devlin Report was shelved happily for everafter.

*And what about the Little Black Banda? They kept him in prison for thirteen months without trial, and then, years later, they all started sending him congratulatory telegrams.*

## A Sequel: Little Lord Monckton

It all started in those far-off bygone days of July 1959. Little Black Banda had been in prison without trial. Lord Justice Devlin had found out the truth about the Government's police state in Nyasaland. 'Singularly unfortunate', cried the Manninghambuller, while the Lennox-Boyd even offered to resign. 'No! No!', said Uncle Mac. 'If at first you don't succeed. . . . Let's have another commission; this time a Royal one. Meanwhile you must continue to show the natives that we really mean business.' And when Uncle Mac and the Lennox-Boyd talked about business they did not mean economic development.

o Uncle Mac searched through all his friends and acquaintances, through all his relations by blood and by marriage for someone he could trust. And there was no one, until one day he remembered Little Lord Monckton, a humble bank clerk slaving away somewhere in the Midlands. Now Little Lord Monckton had never been a High Court Judge; instead, he had been a Tory Cabinet Minister and so he could be trusted. Uncle Mac heaved a sigh of relief and appointed him chairman of the Royal Commission.

here were twenty-five other members; but Uncle Mac wanted to seem to be fair, so he wrote to his chief enemy Uncle Hugh—he wrote because they were only on speaking terms across the floor of the House of Commons—and he said that Uncle Hugh could appoint three of his friends as long as they were Privy Councillors. And Uncle Hugh wrote back that he did not see why they had to be Privy Councillors, that Little Black Banda should be released, and that the Commission should be allowed to consider alternatives to the Federation. Uncle Mac immediately appointed three of *his* friends: Sir Charles Arden-Clarke, Lord Shawcross, the country's youngest elder statesman, and Aidan Crawley.

o, dear, only his friends are allowed to call him creepy Crawley. Only one of these three was a Privy Councillor. As for Little Black Banda, he was kept in prison for a total

of thirteen months without trial, and, despite the fact that Lord Justice Devlin had reported 'that it was generally acknowledged that the opposition to federation was there, that it was deeply rooted and almost universally held', Uncle Mac had persisted in refusing to allow the Commission to consider any alternative to federation.

For a year Little Lord Monckton travelled all over Central Africa. So did happy parties of British MP's enjoying, under the aegis of the Welensky's public relations firm, both sunshine and moonshine. Mr Jenkins, the Tory MP, said that the Welensky had clearly shown himself to be one of the three greatest statesmen of the world today, while Mr Bellenger, who was *meant* to be one of Uncle Hugh's friends, not Uncle Mac's, said that the Federation's continuance was a *sine qua non* for the improvement and advancement of all three territories. The Welensky made a speech about the dangers of intimidation.

In October 1960 Little Lord Monckton's report was published. It called for much more African representation and the end to racial discrimination. It said that the Federation was so unpopular that it would have to be called something else. And most important of all, it recommended that the Government should announce that each territory should have the right to secede. Even a Tory ex-Cabinet Minister cannot be trusted all of the time!

The Welensky was not amused. While claiming that he would not dwell on the gross discourtesy to himself and Uncle Mac, he proceeded to do so in a speech lasting for several hours. But a Conservative's home is his castle in the air and Uncle Mac desperately repeated to the Conservative Party Conference what he had been saying all along. 'The purpose of the Monckton Commission is to help us not to destroy but to confirm and develop the Federal association.' With perhaps more relevance he continued: 'Their Governments, like all governments, will commit follies; their countries, like all countries, may be misled by demagogues. But after all, that happens even among experienced people.' Uncle Jo Grimond was delighted. 'The Monckton Commission's report cannot be pigeon-holed,' he said. But then Uncle Jo was so young and ingenuous that he hardly deserved the title of Uncle.

ncle Hugh wanted to know if the Commission's recommendations would be accepted, but Uncle Mac said that everyone was to wait for the Federal Review Conference. In December 1960 the Conference opened in London; twelve days later, with nothing accomplished, it adjourned for Christmas. We never saw it again.

ince then, Uncle Mac's Butler, who had been reduced to Uncle Mac's odd-job man, has been put in charge of Central African affairs.

n Nyasaland, in August 1961, Little Black Banda, at long last rescued from prison, won 94 per cent of the vote and 22 out of 28 seats. *The Times* said: 'It was the quietest and most orderly election your correspondent has ever witnessed.' In Northern Rhodesia it took more than a year, the resignation of the Marquess of Salisbury from the presidency of the Hertford Conservative Association and three White Papers to impose a constitution. In Southern Rhodesia the United Nations condemned the Government by 81 votes to 2, South Africa and Portugal their faithful chums. The Edgar Whitehead, one of the Welensky's creatures, returned from New York proudly boasting that the Soviet Union had bought a TV film he had made setting out the ideals and hopes of his government.

s recently as last May but one Uncle Hugh and his friends proposed in the House of Commons that 'this House calls upon her Majesty's Government to implement the majority recommendations of the Monckton Commission, and in particular to declare its intention to permit secession by any of the territories in the Central African Federation.' They called for quite a long time before anything happened, and when it did the Welensky suddenly exploded. But whether anyone was going to live happily ever after, was still anybody's guess.

# *ANNABEL*   Keith Waterhouse *&* Willis Hall

AS THE GOVERNMENT reels from one crisis to another it is more and more in need of help. Mr Macmillan, always a keen student of the Press, surely turned his attention to those most rewarding columns of all—the readers' advice pages of the women's magazines?

### FROM HAROLD MACMILLAN

*Dear Annabel,*

I am a Prime Minister and for the last sixteen months I have been having an affair with a French boy named Charles, even though I knew he had other friends. I was persuaded to do what I knew was wrong, and now something that should have happened hasn't happened. But Charles has let me down and wants nothing more to do with me. I am so ashamed. What shall I do?

*Yours,*
*Anxious.*

### FROM PETER THORNEYCROFT

*Dear Annabel,*

I am the Minister of Defence and recently I have been very friendly with a charming American boy named Kennedy. My problem is that I do not know whether he is serious. He keeps making promises and up to now I have always believed him. But other Ministers of Defence have told me that they have been out with American boys too and that they have been jilted. Am I wrong to go on hoping?

*Yours,*
*Undecided.*

*Dear Anxious,*

Oh dear, you are in a pickle, but I am afraid you have no one to blame but yourself. This is the way all these holiday affairs end; you should have had nothing to do with this foreign boy in the first place. Why not find yourself a nice pen-friend in Australia or Canada, or buckle down to some work at home to take your mind off this unhappy affair. As to your present predicament, I am sending you a leaflet which might help you. If you feel embarrassed, why not go to the country?

*Dear Undecided,*

It is unfair of this American boy to lead you on. He must make it clear what his real intentions are and whether he can fulfil his promises. You have not told me his age but from his attitude he sounds immature; perhaps he is not ready to settle down yet. Before you throw him over, however, make sure you have another boy to go to.

FROM HENRY BROOKE

*Dear Annabel,*

I think I am the Home Secretary and my problem is that I lack self-confidence. I am desperately shy, somewhat retiring in nature, and I feel that no one takes any notice of anything I say. The other day I said some quite perceptive things about prisons, but everybody just laughed. Can you help?

*Yours,*
*Hopeless Henry.*

*Dear Hopeless Henry,*

My advice to you is to stop feeling sorry for yourself. Do not moon about the House all day— get out and meet people. It may be difficult at first but persevere. Do not worry about having a retiring nature—people are always retiring in your kind of job.

FROM RICHARD WOOD

*Dear Annabel,*

I am Minister of Fuel and Power and I think I am going out of my mind. My trouble is frigidity. I try so hard not to be cold but all my plans seem to go wrong and when it comes to it I cannot do anything. Should I seek outside help?

*Yours,*
*Frantic.*

*Dear Frantic,*

My guess is that you are over-anxious. Perhaps your wife can help. Why not get her to pose for some more tomfool pictures showing how she personally keeps out the cold. Do not worry too much—many people have your problem.

*To Perplexed, Admiralty.* I do wish you had sent your name and address, for I would like to have written to you privately on this matter. I beg you, have nothing to do with this boy. His offer to take care of blueprints, secret documents, microfilm, etc., does not sound genuine, especially as you tell me he uses after-shave lotion.

ENTITLED TO KNOW       David Nathan & Dennis Potter

*The Conservative pamphlet 'Entitled to Know' caused a stir early in 1963. Based on sentences and half-sentences torn out of Labour Party policy documents and speeches it proved that hundreds of firms are going to be nationalised if—or should it be when—Labour gets into power. Since then Nationalisation has played a smaller part in the campaign. Perhaps the Tories realised that Labour itself can use the same techniques on Tory speeches and pamphlets. Every quote is guaranteed. The people are, as they say, 'Entitled to Know.'*

These meddling, doctrinaire Tories have a dismal record of nationalising everything in sight. In 1887 they first gave *compulsory* powers for the *public* purchase of land. They provided public baths and public post-offices. In 1926 they set up the public Central Electricity Board; in 1933, the London Passenger Transport Act. And then, gorging themselves with a great private industry they *nationalised civil aviation* in 1939 by purchasing Imperial Airways and British Airways to make BOAC. *Why?* The Tory pamphlets explain:

'The development of far-sighted, long-range policy in British aircraft production cannot be attained by private companies. A public corporation can raise capital more cheaply.'

*List of threatened firms:* HANDLEY PAGE, GLOSTER AIRCRAFT CO., SAUNDERS-ROE, ROLLS-ROYCE.

In 1945 the Conservative Party committed itself to a Water Act with *public boards*—and an extension of the Forestry Commission! Ten years later the Tory Government opened Calder Hall and *deliberately extended nationalisation to the field of atomic power stations.* For, as they said:

'Conservatives realise that there is no clear-cut division between Nationalisation and other forms of industrial organisation.'

*Threatened firms:* ANY OTHER FORM OF INDUSTRIAL ORGANISATION e.g. WOOLWORTHS.

In 1945 the Tories also set up a new public authority in Scotland. They called it the South of Scotland Electricity Board.

'These arrangements have considerably improved and strengthened the administration of Scottish affairs.'

*Threatened firms:* HARRIS TWEED, SCOTS PORAGE OATS.

Worse by far, the Tories in their hated National Parks legislation have taken under *public control* various parts of the country. They have taken over the Pembrokeshire Coast, the North Yorkshire Moors, Exmoor and *large parts* of the Yorkshire Dales. As Sir Anthony Eden put it in October, 1954:

'The use of property must be conditioned by the need to preserve the countryside or to secure development for *sound public purposes.*'

*Threatened areas:* LAKE DISTRICT, NEW FOREST, BODMIN MOOR, BOW, etc.

It is, unfortunately, true, that the Labour Party nationalised a few firms . . . but only the dead-beat ones, the failures. The Tories, on the other hand, see these industries as a platform for *yet further advance*. In 1951, for instance, Tory MP's Ted Leather and Harold Watkinson issued a pamphlet full of praise for public ownership.

'Conservatives believe that in the nationalised industries is to be found *an ideal proving ground*, where the Government should pioneer advances in labour relations and management techniques as an *example* and a *spur* to private enterprise.'

Oh, yes. Labour policy offers every man a House and a Car. But the Tories built more *public houses* and then made hissing noises at the *private car*. In February 1962, a Tory document ominously called *Change and Challenge* declared:

'The private car *cannot supersede* public transport. Experience has proved that *free movement* within a town or city is only possible by *public transport*.'

*Threatened firms:* FORD, BMC, ROLLS-ROYCE (again).

And if big companies like Ford think they can wriggle out of that one, let them ponder on this savage Tory remark in a Conservative Political Centre pamphlet of 1950.

'Large undertakings tend by their nature to be bureaucratic . . . when the form of control is out of date and unadaptable, *complete nationalisation* might represent a freeing of endeavour.'

*Threatened firms:* FORD (again), WOOLWORTHS (again), ROLLS-ROYCE (three times).

'Unlike the Labour Party, the Conservative Party would not have a slogan of nationalisation for 30 years and discover, when in office, that there was great difficulty in giving effect to it.'

And that is no idle boast. The Labour Party had been content to nationalise the medical profession, but the *One Nation* Tory pamphlet of 1950 went further.

'The present scheme is not really comprehensive. Many services *have yet* to take *their full part . . . chiropody is an obvious example!*'

And then, in 1954, the Tories set up *public slaughterhouses*.

'The general policy, which will take some years to work out, is to work towards a moderate concentration of *slaughterhouses throughout the country*.'

*Threatened animals:* COWS, SHEEP, PIGS, POULTRY.

Yes, the Tories were getting bloodthirsty all round. Not content with the public slaughter of your meat, the Tory policy document *The Right Road for Britain* demanded a *determined public policy* for the Fishing Industry.

'It is of the greatest *public* importance to preserve the fertility of the fishing grounds. We shall enact legislation to set up a *White Fishmarketing Board*.'

Mac Fisheries, watch out! Bird's Eye Fish Fingers, beware! You have been warned! Tory meddling with private enterprise has a long and sad heritage. Winston Churchill first advocated nationalisation of railways in 1919.

'There is a broadening field for State ownership and enterprise, especially in relation to monopolies of all kinds.'

But this wretched faith is not confined to the past. Lord Hailsham is the voice of

*45*

Toryism rampant, and in his Penguin Special *The Case for Conservatism*—written when he was a Hogg—he makes even more threats.

'The Conservatives have instituted or helped to institute a variety of different forms of public ownership and control which they see no reason to repent of doing. The collection of the variety of forms of public ownership *cannot yet be regarded as complete*.'

What a prospect, ladies and gentlemen! We can, thanks to the Tories, cook our publicly bred fish or publicly slaughtered meat with publicly owned electricity and drive to our publicly owned offices in our publicly owned transport which may soon run on publicly owned atomic power. Or we can walk the publicly owned pavements until our private feet need the attentions of a publicly owned chiropodist or soaking in a bowl of publicly owned water drawn from a publicly owned reservoir in a publicly owned mountain district patrolled by a publicly owned aircraft.

*Set the people free! Labour freedom works! Hands off private industry!*

The enemy's everywhere. Even this was, after all, first broadcast by the publicly owned British Broadcasting Corporation. The Tories did that, too.

*HARDLY HANSARD*    Andrew Roth & Joe Haines

PEOPLE WHO BELIEVE that Hansard is a verbatim report of what goes on in the Houses of Parliament are in for a surprise. One of the chief jobs of a Hansard writer is not so much to write what the member says, as to put right what the member says. Even MP's make mistakes. Even people like Mr Neil McLean (Conservative, Inverness).

'The number of accidents on the M1 has been immensely lower since it was built than before it was built.'

On the same subject, Mr John Farr (Conservative, Hanborough):

'I frequently travel up the M1 by road.'

When this sort of thing happens it poses quite a problem to the editors of the Parliamentary record, Hansard. They may solve it in one of several ways. Sometimes they think the joke good enough to be left to posterity. Mr Harold Davies (Labour, Leek):

'Eggs and milk are their bread and butter!'

Or Mr Tudor Watkins (Labour, Brecon and Radnor):

'What is the answer, that is the question.'

And Hansard has another solution to the difficulties with which it is presented, Sir Barnett Janner (Labour, Leicester NW):

'The boy shot one bird, and had to be destroyed.'

And Mr Robert Woof (Labour, Blaydon) said:

'The future is yet to come.'

Such remarks, in a mood of irritation, or maybe of weariness, Hansard simply deletes. More often the editors solve the problem by a tactful rephrasing of the honourable member's remark. For example, when the harassed Assistant Postmaster-General, Miss Mervyn Pike, said in the House,

'I am sorry there had been a delay in the post, but a committee has been sitting on the mails.'

Hansard altered it to 'committee is at present considering the distribution of mails'. Sometimes a more major reconstruction is involved. The Conservative member for Putney, Sir Hugh Linstead's remark,

'One has only to look round this Chamber to see all the honourable members who are not here.'

appeared in Hansard as: 'It is obvious from looking round the House that Hon. members who are considerably concerned with the details of the Bill, and who would have like to have been here today, have not found it possible to come.'

Great stuff! But now and again an intriguing statement is lost to us completely. The Conservative backbencher who stood up in the Unemployment debate and said:

'With reference to the large areas which I have in my mind. . . .'

and Mr Donald Wade (Liberal, Huddersfield) who said:

'Although I refer to widows it does not mean I am not interested in spinsters.'

Too much for Hansard, both of these. They disappeared. Or, could it have been that they were just tactfully edited to the point where they were no longer recognisable?

# ALDERMASTON    Peter Lewis & Peter Dobereiner

*EASTER WOULDN'T SEEM the same without the knowledge that somewhere, out in the rain, another Aldermaston march is converging on London. As the years go by it becomes more and more one of those lovable British institutions, sandwiched between the distribution of the Maundy Money and Trooping the Colour. What will the scene be like in 1993 when tradition has had time to do its work? One thing is certain: Richard Dimbleby will be there to give commentary.*

. . . We are in Trafalgar Square once again for one of the great ceremonial occasions of the British calendar, the Aldermaston Drive. And there's an enormous crowd, a very excited crowd, waiting here today for the approach of the drivers who have set out more than 15 minutes ago from Piccadilly Circus on the long, fatiguing Aldermaston procession to Trafalgar Square.

Some younger viewers may be wondering why the term Aldermaston is used for this great yearly ritual. It is named, of course, after the obscure Berkshire hamlet where in the earlier years of the century the primitive marchers mustered at the Atomic Weapons Research Establishment, as it was called, long since abandoned for lack of funds. Quite early on the departure point was moved to Hammersmith, where most of the marchers joined the ranks in any case, and later to less remote and outlying districts, such as Kensington, Belgravia, Marble Arch and finally Piccadilly Circus itself. But tradition was not forgotten. Oh no! One token marcher is selected each year to set out all alone from Aldermaston itself, as in the days of our glorious past—and here he comes, yes, that's him entering the square at this moment and this great crowd is going wild with enthusiasm. And the massed bands of the Brigade of Guards are striking up the traditional greeting: 'When the Saint Goes Marching In'.

And following him, now I can see the head of the carriage procession which has been drawn up waiting in the Haymarket. Yes, in the the first carriage, drawn by four greys from the Royal Mews, there is the splendidly mitred figure of Archbishop Collins, blessing the crowd with that symbolic three-fingered gesture with which he is associated. And close behind him, carried on a litter, is that venerable elder statesman, the Lord High Protest, Viscount Foot, wearing purple peer's robes with the holy sign 'Ebbw Vale' worked in ermine across his back—my researchers tell me it refers to a long-forgotten place of martyrdom. And now, coming into the square at the head of his escort of Household Cavalry, is the dazzling uniform of the Transport and General King of Arms, Sir Frank Cousins, KG, KCND, carrying aloft the ceremonial black banner. This is the same banner that has been carried for countless years of our history, patched and worn, with its indecipherable symbols that are believed originally to have had something to do with some sort of protest or other.

And he's trooping the banner! The great banner is slowly and solemnly lowered as Sir Frank rides past the saluting base where Dame Vanessa Redgrave stands ready to read the royal address of welcome. This custom began many years ago when it was discovered that her imitation of the Queen sounded more like the real thing than the Queen herself.

And now we can hear the choir of Westminster Abbey leading this magnificent crowd in the solemn traditional anthem that is always sung on these occasions, called 'Ban The Bloody H-Bomb'. In the early days it was sung to the tune of 'John Brown's Body', but later the Poet Laureate, Sir Alex Comfort, who wrote it, adapted it with the help of the

Master of the Queen's Music, Sir Lionel Bart, Bart., to this early Edwardian traditional air, formerly known as 'Land of Hope and Glory', whose words could no longer be understood by anyone.

And at any moment a great hush will fall on this multicoloured scene as the trumpeters of the Royal Military School of Music sound the Last Post, the signal for the two-minute sit-down. But first, here comes the fly-past, the great fly-past of Bomber Command, consisting of the two famous old V-bombers specially taken out of mothballs for the great day, carrying their two obsolete H-bombs, whose original warheads have been loaned for the occasion by the Victoria and Albert Museum. . . .

I have been asked to interrupt this broadcast for a late news flash from Geneva. 'The 9,674th session of the 82-nation disarmament conference broke up today in total deadlock. A spokesman said: "Absolutely no progress has been made. We are at the position that was reached in 1954."'

I don't see what that's got to do with it. . . .

# BUT MY DEAR     Peter Shaffer

Mr Galbraith declared that he will never again use the words 'Dear' or 'My dear' to begin a letter. In high places in Whitehall the language of all business letters is still being subjected to the most careful examination.

*The scene is an office. A senior official is sitting at his desk; a junior official is quaking nervously as he hands a letter he has just composed to his pompous and bullying senior.*

SENIOR OFFICER: (*Taking the letter*) Give it here. (*Reading*) 'To Mr Jenkins.' Good. None of that 'dear' nonsense. (*Reading*) 'Pursuant to your letter. . .' *Pursuant?*

JUNIOR OFFICER: It's the usual phrase, sir.

SENIOR OFFICER: I don't like it. The word has an erotic penumbra. Take it out.

JUNIOR OFFICER: Yes, sir.

SENIOR OFFICER: (*Reading*) 'I am hoping for the favour of an early reply.' *Favour?*

JUNIOR OFFICER: The Oxford Dictionary defines the verb favour as 'to look kindly upon'.

SENIOR OFFICER: (*Pouncing*) Exactly. I am amazed you can be so naïve. Looking kindly upon anyone who earns less than you do is a deeply treacherous procedure.

JUNIOR OFFICER: I'm very sorry, sir.

SENIOR OFFICER: You need some basic training in modern manners, I can see that. If a man comes 300 miles to see you with papers, keep him waiting in the hall—or better still the drive, if you have one. If you offer him so much as a sandwich you will be suspected of improper relations; and a three-course lunch spells treason.

JUNIOR OFFICER: Yes, sir.

SENIOR OFFICER: You really are an innocent, aren't you?

JUNIOR OFFICER: I'm afraid I am, sir.

SENIOR OFFICER: Well we must change all that. (*Continuing to read*) 'Hoping for the favour of an early reply. . . . *Thanking you in anticipation.*' Are you doing this on purpose?

JUNIOR OFFICER: What, sir?

SENIOR OFFICER: *Thanking you in anticipation.*

JUNIOR OFFICER: Is that wrong, sir?

SENIOR OFFICER: Wrong? It's just about the most sexually provocative sentence I've ever read. It whinnies with suggestiveness.

JUNIOR OFFICER: I hadn't intended it like that, sir.

SENIOR OFFICER: We're not concerned with your intentions, man—merely with the effect you create. And I can tell you that it's nauseating. You have the correspondence style of a lovesick *au pair* girl. In more honest days one would have said kitchen-maid.

JUNIOR OFFICER: But, sir——

SENIOR OFFICER: Don't interrupt, or I may lose control. Now understand this: in the Civil Service you will never thank anybody for anything, especially in anticipation. You will simply end your letter without innuendo of any kind. Now let's see what you've done. (*Reading*) 'Yours faithfully'. . . . I don't believe it.

JUNIOR OFFICER: That's normal, sir.

SENIOR OFFICER: Normal? In the context of a man writing to a man it's nothing less than disgusting. It implies you can be *UN*-faithful!

JUNIOR OFFICER: I never thought of that, sir.

SENIOR OFFICER: You think of very little, don't you? Even the word 'Yours' at the end of a letter is dangerous. It suggests a willingness for surrender.

JUNIOR OFFICER: Then what can I say, sir?

SENIOR OFFICER: What do the Pensions Department use? They're about as unemotional as you can get, without actually being dead.

JUNIOR OFFICER: '*Your obedient servant*', I think.

SENIOR OFFICER: Are you mad?

JUNIOR OFFICER: Sir?

SENIOR OFFICER: *Your obedient servant.* . . . That's just plain perverted. People who want to be other people's obedient servants are the sort who answer those advertisements: Miss Lash, ex-Governess of striking appearance. To sign yourself an obedient servant is an *ipso facto* confession of sexual deviation. And *that*, as we all know, is an *ipso facto* confession of treason.

JUNIOR OFFICER: Oh, I say, sir!

SENIOR OFFICER: What do you say? (*Looking at him narrowly*) I believe you are one of those cranks who believe that there are loyal homosexuals! (*Accusingly*) I think you secretly believe that the way to stop homosexuals being blackmailed into subversive acts is to change the law so they can't be.

JUNIOR OFFICER: Well, it had crossed my mind, sir. Amend the law and the possibility of Vassalls is lessened.

SENIOR OFFICER: Sloppy, left-wing sentimentality! The only way to stop a homosexual being blackmailed is to stop him being a homosexual. And the only way you can do that is to lock him up in a building with five hundred other men. That way he can see how unattractive they really are. Now take this pornographic muck out of here and bring it back in an hour, clean enough to be read by a six-year-old girl, or John Gordon. And leave out everything at the end except your name: a bare signature, brusque and masculine. What is your name, by the way?

JUNIOR OFFICER: Fairy, sir.

SENIOR OFFICER: I don't think somehow you are going to go very far in Her Majesty's Service. Good morning.

# FIVE-YEAR TESTS    Gerald Kaufman

FIVE-YEAR-OLD motor cars are no longer allowed to travel on the Queen's Highway without having passed a road-worthiness test. By the decision of MP's, tests for brakes, lights and steering are becoming compulsory for more and more cars. But what if MP's themselves had to undergo brakes, lights and steering tests?

These were the results of the latest Westminster-worthiness tests.

*Mr Harold Lever: Labour MP for Cheetham.* Is noted for his filibustering speeches —he spoke for two-and-a-quarter hours on the Cinematograph Film Production Bill and for two-and-a-half hours on the White Fish and Herring Industries Bill.

*Weak spot:* brakes. Their tendency to jam over long distances makes this vehicle an obstacle to other would-be road-users.

*Mr Alan Brown: MP for Tottenham.* Elected as a Labour MP. Has now joined the Conservatives, and will be opposed by a Labour candidate at the General Election.

*Weak spot:* steering. This vehicle was designed for driving on the left hand side of the road. But a basic structural flaw causes it to lurch over to the right, and it will now operate only on that side of the road. We recommend that it be withdrawn from service.

*Mr Selwyn Lloyd: Conservative MP for the Wirral.* Was responsible for the stop-go-stop-go economic policy, and the guiding light wages policy. Dismissed from the Government in July 1962, and has since taken charge of inquiries into Conservative Party organisation and footballers' wages.

*Weak spot:* This vehicle has now been taken out of service on main roads and is held in reserve for light, inessential duties. This was a wise decision, since otherwise it would have been necessary to recommend that it be placed in the House of Lords museum of old crocks.

*Mr Michael Foot: Labour MP for Ebbw Vale.* He was elected as a Labour MP, but the party whip was withdrawn from him and he sat as an Independent. Now he is Labour again.

*Weak spot:* steering. This low-slung racing model travels so rapidly that, with its ineffectual steering mechanism, it invariably veers over to the extreme left of the road and ends up in the ditch. It also backfires alarmingly. Unless this vehicle can be made more responsive to control, the insurance authorities will refuse to accept it for third-party risk.

*Mr Ernest Marples: Minister of Transport. Weak spots:* brakes, lights and steering. Once it starts, this vehicle cannot be stopped—whatever the hazard to pedestrians. Its steering is so erratic that even the driver has no idea which way it is going. The lights cannot be turned off—indeed the vehicle is unable to operate unless illuminated with full spotlights. In addition, the horn is jammed; it never stops blowing. This vehicle simply is not up to the demands made on it. It should be replaced by a bicycle.

*BUDGET DAY*     Nathan & Potter

**He may be Chancellor of the Exchequer**

**but he can't tell Stork from butter**

3246098 L/CPL WALLACE, A., ROYAL SIGNALS. INDEPENDENT.

GOOD EVENING TO YOU. I am speaking to you tonight from the gas-cape store at Kitchener Lines, No. 14 Supply Depot, Uttoxeter, at a time when Britain is at the cross-roads of history and our fate is in the balance. Right?

I have been excused all duties this evening in order to acquaint you with my programme for the critical years ahead. Right then. Why should you—the Bri'ish civvies—support an Army candidate in preference to a—er—Bri'ish civvy? Right then. The first and primary thing to remember at all times is, No. 1, you play ball with me and I'll play ball with you; No. 2, me and some of the lads here often have recourse to sit down the Naafi chatting each other up about the world situation and that. Out of our sessions we have formed a Shadow Cabinet of volunteers ready and willing to come forward and have a crack at running the country. You do not know until you have tried. Mr Wilson and his trade-union bashers may think they can do better than us. Our message to Mr Wilson tonight is, *Get some time in.*

Policy. What is our policy? It is as follows. Right? No. 1: Commonwealth.

Our Shadow Secretary for Commonwealth Affairs is Provost-Sergeant Macmichael, J., who has done extensive tours of the Commonwealth and is in fact married to a wog bint.

So what Jock does not know about these hot countries is not worth knowing; get your knees brown, Lord Home.

No. 2: Afri'a.

Our Shadow Colonial Secretary, Signalman Cooney, who is himself an Anglo-Banglo, proposed to go on a goodwill mission to all these nignog countries and chat up the blackies as if they was man to man. As Signalman Cooney so shrewdly puts it, you've got to live with the darkies, therefore you might as well look as if you was good mates—and I endorse this policy.

Policy No. 3: Common Market.

I would like to introduce to you tonight, our European expert, Fusilier Geordie Woolerton.

Without swinging the lamp, Geordie has had more hours in Minden than Mr Heath has had hot dinners. He outlines our Common Market Policy quite simply and succinctly: You cannot trust the Krautheads. Also, if the price of a bottle of lager at Helga's bar, Windelstrasse, is indicative of Common Market trading, you can stuff it.

Turning to Home Affairs, on the vexed question of taxation and allowances, our Shadow Chancellor of the Exchequer is Officers' Cook Maloney.

Paddy Maloney, as he is known affectionately to his colleagues, will iron out the many anomalies in our economy. Why, for example, should a Technical Sergeant get more than a Cook Sergeant?

As my late meal chitty expires very shortly indeed, I have no time to go in detail into our other policies, as for example, get the nancy-boys out of security jobs, smarten up the Yank troops, and stop the Guards working as servants in Lords' houses, why should they?

To you the Bri'ish Civvies I say vote for me and you can't go far wrong.

And to my fellow squaddies trying to work it out of the mob, I say, come and join your Oppo's.

It's a Man's life in the Bri'ish Government Today; I thank you.

# 3 Sport

*THE OPEN ROAD*    Keith Waterhouse & Willis Hall

GERALD MOONEY, *a modest accountant from Beckenham, Kent, sitting in an invalid wheel-chair, one arm in a sling and a bandage round his head, speaks in the droning delivery of a man who has had a severe shock to his system.*

Nineteen-sixty-two had all the promise of a full and happy year for me. I had secure employment as an accountant in Beckenham, Kent. I was the proud possessor of a 1,000 c.c. four-door saloon in beige. Alas and alack, those rosy days are gone and I face nineteen-sixty-three the broken man you see before you now.

It is true that I like a drink. Admittedly. But, moderation in all things, and when the slogan 'If you drink don't drive—if you drive don't drink' came to my attention, naturally I endorsed it.

That was in the period January to November. In December the rot set in. One Saturday evening, in company with my wife, I sat watching that reputable programme Dixon of Dock Green. At the end of the story, a happy tale about an old-age pensioner who was a bit of a character, P.C. George Dixon himself took leave to address us, his audience. 'If you're going to a party', said he, 'take a tip from me and leave your car at home.' Three hours later, I was still in front of my set when who should come before us but Mr Marples himself. After outlining a plan to build a system of tunnels and flyovers embracing the whole of the British Isles, Mr Marples ended on a typically philosophical note: 'When Mrs Marples and I go to a party, either she drinks and I drive, or I drive and she drinks. Good motoring to you all.'

Now in all my years as a motorist no one has ever asked me to a party. I have never been to a party in my life—with or without my car.

Who organises these parties? The RAC? The Automobile Association? Does my local garage hold cocktail parties for the regular customers? If so why am I not on the list? Are the service areas halfway up the M1 filled far into the night with wild Bacchanalian cries and shouts of 'One for the road'? If so, such revelries are exclusively for owners of Jags and Thunderbirds and not for the likes of me. Does the Secretary of my local car rally hold an At Home on New Year's Eve? I rang him up and asked him and he was cagey to say the least.

Furthermore, where do Mr and Mrs Marples get to every night?

Was there something wrong with me? Was it me or was it my car?

I decided to find out. Late last night I drove off to the Kingston By-pass and clocked up thirty-five miles while cruising up and down in search of advanced motorists in a state of advanced intoxication. Midnight found me in the Roehampton area and stone-cold sober. I pulled in carefully to the side of the road, switched on my parking light and began to sob quietly to myself over the wheel. Who knows how long I sat there? In the small hours of the morning a crowd of drunken pedestrians, all of whom had left their cars at home, came whooping past and saw me weeping. 'Ho-ho!' they cried gleefully. 'A drunken motorist! It is up to us to teach him a lesson!'

It was the work of a moment for them to turn my car over and me in it. One of them broke a bottle of whisky over my head, and thus it was that, reeking of drink, I was hauled from the wreckage and arrested. I appear at Bow Street tomorrow and will probably go to prison. The gregarious Mr and Mrs Marples, on the other hand, go scot free. Not to mention P.C. Dixon and Co. The moral of my tale is: If you wish to drink and drive you must have friends.

# Guilty Man Probe Must Go—Podd

## Police Clash in Quant Race Swoop

### From David Frost & Peter Cook

DATELINE: ROME

**On the red shale track, it was a black, black day of gloom, despair and despondency for the British lads and lassies who ran their hearts into the ground in the sizzling cauldron that is Rome. *Rome? I prefer to call it the muddle city of all time.***

### FLOUNDERING

In the farcically-run 10,000 metres, the British contingent, upset by the sounds of Italian love-making in their near-by cubicles, looked tired and drawn at the start.

Twenty-eight-year-old lion-hearted Big Dick Podd, burly high hurdler and Sussex nacksmith, turned to reporters: 'I am in the wrong race', he revealed.

*But* minutes later Big Dick was floundering in the rear, lapped in the first fifteen seconds by the Polish Ace, Grobotski.

'I admit I was beaten fair and square,' confessed Big Dick, flushed with defeat. 'But what can you do when you're up against a Pole?'

Full of Yorkshire grit, Dorothy Quant, plucky mother of three, did *not* agree. Away to a good start in the 200 metres, she immediately made a quick spurt for the winners' rostrum, only to be manhandled away by swarthy Italian militia.

### A SMEAR

Meanwhile, in a seething Rome—Rome? I prefer to call it the Terrazzo of Tittle-Tattle—rumours fly like bees round a glass of milk.

What has big Mary Smallcot to say about the smear that has been laid at her door?

'I think it's all a lot of——' wheezed our golden two-day yachting hope.

'*If the British girls are men, then I'm a Dutchman*', declared prominent Amsterdam businessman Hugo Van Der Huyst.

Said twenty-nine-year-old bespectacled London solicitor Allan Broth:

'*Epee? It's a mystery to me, but if it's a question of letting the old country down, I'm willing to have a go.*' (Wilfred Pickles, please note.)

### HOLOCAUST

British hopes were pinned high on the frail, pain-racked form of one-time bookie's runner Tim ('Call me Mr Tompkins') Tompkins, trained to a peak by stateless architect Heinrich Gestetner, the mysterious German behind Britain's failure in the track events.

Gestetner, incidentally, went to school with the Duke of Edinburgh, but that was before the outbreak of the ghastly war, which was to overwhelm Europe, and bring an end to organised athletics as we knew it.

The sweltering British fans many of whom had paid out some of their own money to see the so-called Games, could ill-disguise their disappointment as Tompkins failed to start.

'I tracked the wrong man,' he stormed thoughtfully, brushing aside reporters. 'But watch the feathers fly in Tokyo.'

*Well, you've said it, Mr Tompkins.*

### POCK SPEAKS

Brian Pock, seven-year-old teenage diving sensation, was adamant.

'In the days of the Roman Empire, when Justinian ran the length of the Marathon to greet his wife Poppaea, there was no question of athletes asking for 6d. a week pocket money,' he vouchsafed.

'But in an age of atomic submarines and all-purpose plastics, Britain must, if she is to maintain her position among the magic fourteen European diving nations, pour £48m. into new heated boating rinks up and down our green and pleasant land.'

On the sunbaked Soccer fields of Rome—Rome? I prefer to call it Sodom and Gomorrah in sheep's clothing —British prestige sunk to yet another all-time low.

### PANTIES

*It was not sufficient for luckless Goalie Finn to point to the Tower of Pisa and say, 'Even the great must take a tumble'.*

This Britishsoccerbluesday —there is no other word for it —drove another nail into the tottering coffin of Britain's Barons of Ball and Caliphs of Kick, who, if they do not yield to the public demand for a floodlit Asian Super-League, must surely kiss goodbye to Alf Ramsey and his pipe-dreams of a world Soccer-garchy.

More chaos from the Pentathlon pit. Said nineteen-year-old American negress, Wilma Horse, 'The Swedish pantie raids put a spanner in my works, and did nothing to lift the air of gloom that hung like a pall over the Olympic Village'.

## PETITE PATATO

Pat Milk ('Petite Patato' as she is known to the hordes of Italian hangers-on who seem to infest this city) putting up four pounds overweight on Dusky Pasha, unseated Italian D'Inzi in the world of leather and flying hoof.

'*These greasy wops have put me in the Pudding Club*', she roared as she passed the Judges' stand.

*BUT* let the last word be with the British team-boss, Jack Podd. 'It was the low quality and poor condition of our athletes that was responsible for our defeats. Nothing else.'

**That's as may be, Mr Slicktalk Podd, but all the words in the world can't wash away the taste of defeat, disaster, humiliation and abject horror that was Rome, 1963, 1964, 1965, etc. etc.**

## FOOTBALLER'S PROGRESS

Brian Glanville

And now we are going to bring you Johnny Pitts, Rovers' brilliant young centre-forward, to show you what put the star quality into this young soccer star, to show you the men—and the women—who made him what he is today.

First a word from the man who found Johnny, ace talent scout Dickie Sludge.

'The minute I saw John go round five men, flick the ball over the goalkeeper's head and walk it into the net, I said to myself, this boy is going to make it.'

But before he went, Sludge had to convince Johnny's wise old working-class, salt-of-the-earth father, Reggie Pitts, a part-time parking-meter attendant from Balham, that Johnny was doing the right thing. As for Johnny himself . . .

didn't want to go out of
e bleeding town, I mean,
made me, the old man
did. . . .'

At Rovers, manager Charlie Art-
ful helped Johnny along the road
to football fame with constant
good advice

Then there was the club coach,
George Marbles, who polished
the rough edges off Johnny's
game.

'This week, lads, we'll be facing an interlock-
ing, zonal, retreating defence, with the
environmental awareness to counteract any
blind-side passing. The only way you'll get
round their screening is with wall passes,
plenty of positive running and using your
peripheral vision.'

Johnny was scoring goals now and the press
were beginning to take notice. He even won
the praise of Peter Fullsome, the loudest
voice in Sunday Soccer.

his zippy youngster brought a cheer from
Fullsome throat when he thundered past
Birmingham defenders and hammered
leather past a helpless Pargeter.'

Johnny also won the approval of bluff, genial chairman
Sam Prong, a local fish-
monger.

'Ay, the lad's got ability,
I'm not denying it. If he
does what he's told and
behaves himself, I think
he'll make a player.'

In Johnny's second season with the Rovers, bluff, genial fishmonger Sam Prong was elected to the England Selection Committee and, by a happy coincidence, this was the season that Johnny first played for his country.

The Chairman of the Selectors himself came to watch Johnny. Wise, far-seeing Joe Geriatric, a man steeped in the wisdom of the game. It was Geriatric's deciding vote on which Johnny's place in the England team depended.

'What did you say his name was, Nitts? Is that him, that one there, the goalkeeper? He's a good player, isn't he, this player, Flitts? That's what I *said*: Titts. What? Oh, he's the *other* centre-forward.'

Johnny was in. His very first game for England. Naturally, like any young lad, he was overjoyed by the honour of wearing his country's shirt for the first time.

'Yeah, well I mean to say, fifty quid; I mean you can't sneeze at it, can you?'

Johnny was lucky in the many good friends he made in the game.

'You leave it to me, John boy; you let me 'a the tickets, send me as many as you can, a when I've flogged them I'll bring you yo cut at the next home game.'

It was about this time that romance came into Johnny's life, in the shape of Helen Higgins, a loyal Rovers' fan.

'I never miss a match, honestly. I've been all round the country with the team and the team's been all over the place with me.

'The first time I saw John, I thought he was lovely; I did really. I'd stand there rattling me rattle and hoping that he'd notice me.

'Then they voted Queen of the S porters' Club, an sold him a ticket the raffle.'

'I didn't know what I was winning and all.'

It was star columnist Peter Full-some who revealed the story of their romance.

'"Reg," cracked Johnny, as I unlocked the door of their honeymoon suite, "this is tougher than scoring goals."'

But Johnny's fame had spread and it wasn't long before the famous agent Giorgio Fanullone appeared, charged by Pro Macaroni, Foggia, to get Johnny's signature at all costs.

But the last word, of course, lay with Helen Pitts.

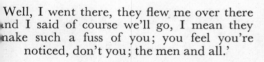

'Well, I went there, they flew me over there and I said of course we'll go, I mean they make such a fuss of you; you feel you're noticed, don't you; the men and all.'

And so they went: to Italy, to the beauties of the Renaissance; to sun, to wine, to music; Johnny felt it was a challenge he couldn't resist; he felt he *had* to go.

'Yeah, well I mean I'd sold me memoirs in advance, hadn't I?'

# 4 Levin

ON THE DEATH OF HUGH GAITSKELL, JAN. 19th 1963

THE SMALLEST PERSONAL contact with Hugh Gaitskell was sufficient to destroy the mythical picture of him as a remote intellectual and to replace it with a true understanding of what was an immensely warm and generous nature. Unhappily, it was only towards the end of his life that this true picture began to assume complete shape in the general public consciousness, just as it was only in the closing stages of his career that his full stature was widely recognised. The irony of his death was that, denied the full range of achievements that were at last in sight for him, he will be mainly remembered, politically speaking, for his success in maintaining, without any compromise of his integrity, a fragile unity of his Party dependent upon his own irreplaceable leadership.

There were three great crises in Hugh Gaitskell's political career, and each of them brought out a different, vital aspect of his character. In the first, the long-drawn duel with Aneurin Bevan, it was those qualities of unshakeable dignity and scrupulous rectitude that were so noticeable, and which must have added much to the profoundly genuine pleasure he took in the fact that that struggle ended in reconciliation.

The second crisis was the storm that racked the Labour Party after the electoral defeat of 1959, in which he displayed, to an extent that only became fully apparent in retrospect, qualities of calmness and foresight that enabled him to keep his head when all around him were urging him to lose it.

The third and greatest crisis was the struggle provoked by the split in the Labour Party over defence policy. And that brought out the trait which was perhaps most characteristic of him—his courage. At the apogee of that struggle (the Labour Party Conference of 1960 at Scarborough), he made a speech, perhaps the greatest of his career, in which he used a phrase that has since almost become part of the fabric of our political language, when he vowed to 'fight, and fight, and fight again'. But the words with which he followed that phrase, and the context in which they were set, have been too readily forgotten. 'There are some of us', he said, 'who will fight, and fight, and fight again, to bring back this Movement into the paths of sanity and dignity, and to save the party we love.'

That he *did* save the party he loved was not the least of his achievements. The tragedy is that it was to be the last. And the tragedy is not his alone, but the tragedy of all those involved in, or even affected by, the struggle for freedom and social justice, those twin causes in which he so devoutly believed, and in the selfless service of which he lived and died.

'The ideals of democratic socialism', he said, as he conceded defeat on Election night in 1959, 'have never shone so brightly.' If they shine less brightly today than yesterday, it is because of his passing.

IT HAS OFTEN BEEN SAID, without the speaker giving much real thought to what he is saying, that the world is being increasingly run by the old, and that many of the tensions and frustrations felt by the young are the result of this. It is natural that every generation should be impatient of its elders, yet I think that today, more than ever before, there is justice in the claim of the young.

One thinks first of the age of the statesmen in whose hands the world and its safety, at any rate nominally, rest. Recent criticism of Mr Macmillan's leadership has not, it is true, concentrated very much on his age; yet who can doubt that, at 75, the Tory leader is not quite as alert, as quick and decisive, as he was at, say, 69? The years of the legendary Dr Adenauer, at 91, are a standing joke, and those of President de Gaulle (86), scarcely less so; yet is there not an unseen and unintended humour in the continual harping on the youth of the 57-year-old President Kennedy, or the 55-year-old Harold Wilson?

It must not be too readily assumed that years alone must necessarily unfit a man for the highest office or its responsibilities. The 83-year-old Verwoerd, and the 79-year-old Kruschev, whatever we may think of their policies, show no signs of failing powers; Mr de Valera, at 97, Dr Salazar at 98, Lord Hailsham at 80 and Mr Hugh Carleton Greene at 81 have all shown, in their different ways, the strength and durability of their faculties; and Alderman Cyril Hopcraft still, at 107, carrying out with aplomb his duties as Chairman of the Watch Committee of Market Harborough Borough Council.

The fact remains, however, that in a world of increasing tensions, operating at an ever-increasing speed, the gravest dangers may lurk in the very advanced age of so many of those in authority. In this country, for instance, few would be so bold as to deny the importance and significance in our national life of the Bench of Bishops; yet their average age is, alarmingly, 87; and if we exclude the comparatively youthful Woolwich (68), Southwark (66), and Bath and Wells (70), the average rises to $89\frac{1}{4}$.

Those of aggressively secular temperament may deny the importance of Bishops; not even they, however, can profess to be happy about the similar—nay, far worse—situation that exists among the judiciary. That the Lord Chief Justice, Lord Parker, is 85, is perhaps not to be entirely regretted; it might be said that the formal head of the judiciary should be a man of venerable years and aspect. But it is enough to give even the most sanguine cause for perturbation to realise that the average age of the judges of the High Court is well over 90. (The precise figure cannot be determined, as several of them were born before the registration of births was made compulsory.) Of course, it does not follow that a man in his tenth decade will necessarily dispense justice any worse than a younger man; and one must certainly admit that the vigour, not to say relish, with which the 99-year-old Mr Justice Gorman sent Miss Barbara Fell to prison for two years for falling in love with a Yugoslav would have done credit, or something, to a man one-third of his age. Mr Justice Gorman, however, is an exception; I am assured by those who have studied him that the half-smile invariably to be found on his lips when he is recommending permanent transportation to Tasmania for an offender charged with leaving his car unattended, shows that this is merely a pleasantry and that his Lordship knows well that the savage penalties current when he was in his prime have long since been swept away. But that this is not true of all his colleagues can scarcely be doubted; one has only to recall the unfortunate incident of last October, when the 94-year-old Mr Justice Merriman imposed the death penalty on a man accused (and, for that matter, acquitted) of selling unstamped eggs, to realise that. (The incident bears out my argument in a striking fashion; for arrangements had been put in hand for the execution, the 98-year-old Governor of Pentonville most excited at the prospect of his first 'topping' since that of Sir Roger Casement, and only the intervention of the 80-year-old Home Secretary, Mr Henry Brooke, whose sole concern was to see that the House of Commons should be properly misled when the 88-year-old Speaker finally allowed discussion, *ex post facto*, of the execution, led to the error being discovered. And even then the 92-year-old Chief Commissioner of Police was reluctant to admit that any mistake had been made.)

In the field of education (surely one in which the gap between the young and their leaders should be as narrow as possible) the situation is, if anything, worse. The average age of University Vice-Chancellors is 82, of the Headmaster's Conference 78, and of the last six Ministers of Education 77. (And this last figure would be considerably higher if it were not for the fact that Sir Edward Boyle at 49 brings the average down substantially, though it is on the other hand true that Dame Florence Horsburgh, who was finally persuaded to relinquish the post at the age of 98, puts it substantially up.)

Newspapers? A sufficient comment is the fact that the youngest editor in Fleet Street, Mr Hugh Cudlipp, is 68, while Lord Beaverbrook is of course well into his nineties. Business? Lord Chandos, President of the Institute of Directors, was strongly criticised at the last Annual General Meeting of that body for rash and impulsive decisions during the year, but was generally excused on the grounds of his youth. He is 83. The Arts? The average age of the members of the Board of the National Theatre is 73, while even Mr Sean Kenny, confidently tipped as the architect of the proposed building, is surely past the first flush of his youth at 52.

One could multiply examples indefinitely—though perhaps one might waggishly suggest that it would be better to subtract examples! But the general pattern is all too clear. This is an old man's country, and getting more so. The complaint of the young is fully justified. In the seventh decade of the twentieth century, it is simply not good enough that the maximum age for joining the Young Conservatives should be 50, the Boy Scouts 40, and the Brownies 35. Nothing short of a widespread and carefully planned programme of euthanasia will meet the case, and no fitter man to draw up and supervise the details of such a programme could possibly be found than Professor Glanville Williams, President of both the Euthanasia Society and the Society for Abortion Law Reform, seemingly a man who believes in burning the candle at both ends, both before and after the horse has flown. He is 90.

# THERE IS NO SUCH BOOK AS 'PARADISE LOST'

I BEGIN THUS *in media res* because the thesis I have to advance is so startling that there is no point in trying to break it gently. The simple truth is, there is no such book as *Paradise Lost*, and what is more there never has been.

If anyone doubts it, let him ask himself a question. Let him ask it privately of himself, when he is alone, and when nothing turns upon the answer, and there is no need to repeat the answer to anybody else. The question is, of course: Have you ever read *Paradise Lost?* The answer will be no. *Nobody* has ever read *Paradise Lost*. Almost everybody has at some time pretended to have read *Paradise Lost*, but nobody has actually done so. They cannot have; for the book does not exist. It is true that if you go into a library, say, or a bookshop that stocks the classics, you will find upon the shelves various editions of a book labelled *Paradise Lost*, by John Milton. And it is equally true that if you open one of these volumes at the first page, you will find a work beginning

> Of Man's first Disobedience, and the Fruit
> Of that Forbidden Tree . . .

You may read on, wondering what on earth I am talking about. But about line 38 ('Of rebel Angels by whose aid aspiring . . .') the reader will be struck, if he is quick-witted, by the realisation that he has not so far understood one word of the proceedings, that there have so far been only two full stops and the same number of main verbs, and that he would much rather be watching television. Certain tougher individuals may struggle on for a few more lines, perhaps getting as far as line 56 (' . . . round he throws his baleful eyes'), before giving up. And I believe that one or two readers have managed to get as far as line 75 ('Oh, how unlike the place from whence they fell!') before collapsing into neurasthenia. There are, as it happens, a further thirty-four lines: the work ends on line 109—a singularly meaningless line, reading 'And what is else not to be overcome?'

And that is all. That is all there is, and all there ever has been, of Milton's *Paradise Lost*. What, then, of the innumerable editions that one can find in shop and library? They are all part of the gigantic Exegetical Conspiracy, a fraud on an unprecedented scale, organised by the academic world for its benefit. The remaining pages of all the books labelled 'Paradise Lost' consist of gibberish, words put down in any order to fill out the lines, excerpts from dictionaries, phone-books, cookery-books, manuals of instruction enclosed with electrical apparatus, the Bible (a very popular source, this last), and anything else the particular editor can lay his hands on to disguise the fact that there is no such work as the one of which he is supposed to be producing yet another uncalled-for and unwanted edition. For the beauty and simplicity of the scheme is self-evident; the editors are perfectly safe from detection, for nobody is capable of reading more than a hundred lines at the very most of the work. When our patience, anywhere between line 2 and line 60, say, is totally exhausted, we simply throw the book aside and pretend for the rest of our lives, like all the other liars, that we have read *Paradise Lost*. Indeed, we may even go so far, to lend credence to the deception, as to quote it. *It is a rarely-observed but undeniable fact that all the quotations from 'Paradise Lost' are from the first 81 lines of Book One.*

When I read a paper along these lines to the Royal Society of Literature, loud jeering and laughter broke out at this point. I countered with a direct question to each member in turn as to whether he was willing to swear an oath to the effect that he had read the work right through. The chairman immediately closed the meeting; an action which speaks for itself. But in those days I was only at the beginning of what has since proved to be not only the most absorbing study I have ever immersed myself in, but the most startling. For I realised, as soon as I began to pursue my researches on any systematic scale, that I had hardly scratched the surface of the immense deception that has been practised on the world for centuries.

The staggering truth is that I have already discovered well over 150 major works of literature which do not exist. They include *Paradise Regained*, of course, of which there are in fact only two lines. But they also include works of hallowed reputation, whose names are on the lips of every literate man and woman, every one of them too weak to admit that they have never done more than glance at the first few lines of the works which, although supposed to be the literary heritage of the world, are too boring for anyone to get through more than a page or two in any circumstances. I give below a partial list, together with some indication of what really exists of these works.

*Canterbury Tales:* Chaucer (The Prologue).

*The Aeneid:* Virgil (First 40 lines of Book One: First 12 lines of Book Ten).

*Complete Works:* Goethe (Act One of Faust, Part One. All the rest of all editions of Goethe's works are in fact blank pages, no living man having ever opened any one of them.)

*The Divine Comedy:* Dante. (The first line of the Inferno. All the rest consists of padding and gibberish; the Dorothy Sayers edition, rather piquantly, merely reprints her detective stories. That the line 'Lasciate ogni speranza, voi che entrate' occurs in the work is a popular legend with no foundation in fact, rather like the belief that 'God tempers the wind to the shorn lamb' is a quotation from the Bible.)

*The Brothers Karamazov:* Dostoievsky. (As far as I can discover, the only part of this work that exists is the title.)

*Parliamentary Practice:* Erskine May. (Again, nothing but the title. When the Speaker of the House of Commons pretends to be consulting it, he is merely reading comics tucked inside an old edition of Bradshaw.)

*The Dialogues:* Plato (First few pages of *The Republic*: the *Death of Socrates* is, of course, a modern pastiche by Arthur Machen.)

*Poetics* and *Politics:* Aristotle (Titles only).

*Social Contract:* Rousseau (First sentence).

*Remembrance of Things Past:* Proust (Book One of *Swann's Way*, up to the *second* mention of the cake. All other volumes of all editions are in fact cigarette-boxes.)

*Marlborough:* Winston Churchill (the maps).

And the complete works of Spinoza, Langland, de Musset, Adam Smith, Matthew Arnold, Beaumont and Fletcher, Cicero, Borrow, Calderon, all the Brontes (with the exception of *Jane Eyre*, which was written by Branwell), Malthus, Nietzsche, Lessing (Gotthold Ephraim, that is, not Doris), Spenser (there never was even such a person as Spenser, let alone such a book as *The Faery Queen*), Whitman, Mickiewicz, St Augustine, Beddoes, Juvenal, Camoens, Schiller and Jung.

And this, as I say, is only a partial selection. But if anyone is disposed to challenge the truth of my revelations, let him try the test I proposed at the beginning for *Paradise Lost*. Have you ever read a word of Schiller? Have you ever opened the works of Spinoza? Have you ever seen a copy of *The Faery Queen*? Do you know anything whatever of the works of Jung apart from what you read in the *Observer*? Have you ever heard of Camoens, and if you have, did you know that his chief work was called *The Lusiads*, and if you do, can you say what a Lusiad is?

Yes the cowardice of men in this modern age, who are afraid to appear less cultured than their fellows, ensures that the conspiracy goes undetected, and the editors, book-reviewers, publishers and the rest of the get-rich-quick crowd can continue to batten on cultural snobbery and human weakness. Nor have I any real hope that my exposure will be taken seriously, let alone that it will bring the whole fraud to an end. I will be dismissed as a jester, and everything will go on as before. So be it. I am content to know what I know, and as for the irony of the situation, I can relish that, too. Isn't there a line somewhere in *Beowulf* that sums up the situation?

## *APOCRYPHAL*

NOW IT CAME TO PASS that men spake dark things of one of the Elders of the land, saying 'He hath lain with harlots', and 'He is an evil-doer', and 'He swimmeth not in the sea after the fashion of other men, but far from the shore, and he fisheth in strange waters'. And all men spake thus behind their hands, and the land was filled with rumour, and the rumours came unto the ears of the highest and the lowest; but the rumours came not unto the ears of Hail, son of Sham, for he stopped his ears against them, that he might not hear the evil things that men were saying against his brother, yea, against his very friend, and that he might continue to sit at the right hand of God, and give advice unto God, and to be not as other men, but holy and virtuous, that all men might sing his praises. And all men did not sing his praises, whereat was his heart sore, and he gave yet more advice unto God. And God took it not.

And it came to pass that the dark things that men spake of the Elder were spoken privily and in darkness, whereat certain persons took counsel together and said 'Wherefore are these things hid?' and 'Why speaketh no man by day what all men speak by night?' And they girded up their loins and spake the things by day, and in a loud voice, and in the market-place, and all men heard the things that all men had already heard, whereat many wondered why these things had thus been spoken, and comforted themselves, saying 'Lo, we knew these things, but Hail, son of Sham, knew them not, and stopped his ears against them, that they might not come unto his ears, and that he might be righteous and upright for evermore, and be worthy to give advice unto God, and to sit at God's right hand. And it is good that these things be now spoken in a loud voice, that they may come at last unto the ears of Hail, son of Sham, that he may walk no longer in the darkness of ignorance, but may walk in the paths of knowledge, and be still holy and virtuous, and upright and righteous, and give advice unto God, whether God taketh it or not. And peradventure that is why these things were spoken in a loud voice, and by day, and in the market-place.'

But when the words were spoken by day, and in a loud voice, and in the market-place, the Council of the Elders took fright, and shook, and were as men who had seen visions, and spake together, and said 'Lo, now all men will know the things that have been spoken of our brother, yea, of our very friend. And men will say that we knew these things to be true, and spake it not. And none shall deliver us from our peril, nay, not Hail, son of Sham, who giveth advice unto God, even though God taketh it not.'

And after they had taken counsel together, they chose five of their number, and bade them go aside, and call unto them the Elder of whom the dark things were spoken, and to ask him if these things were true, or false, and to be sure that he said they were false. So they met privily by night, and summoned to them that Elder, and he rose, and put on his raiment, and went by night, and was admitted unto their presence by a back way. And they sat, and questioned him, saying 'Hast thou lain with harlots?' and 'Art thou an evil-doer?' And he was about to speak, and to say that verily he had lain with harlots, and was an evil-doer, and to beat his breast, and to proclaim that he was a sinner. But they stopped his mouth, saying 'Before thou speakest, hear us.' And he fell silent, as they bade him, and hearkened unto them. And they spoke after this wise.

'Lo, all men say that thou hast lain with harlots, and art an evil-doer, and it is spoken by day, and in the market-place, and in a loud voice, and all men hear it, yea, even Hail, son of Sham, heareth it, and his heart is sore, and giveth confused advice unto God. And it is not only spoken, but written also; it is written every day, and on the Sabbath day is it written twice. And men would not be so bold to say and write these things if they were not true. And men say that there are epistles of thine to thy harlots, wherein thou speakest to her with honeyed words, and with endearments, and these epistles have some of our number seen, and it is true that thou speakest therein with honeyed words and with endearments. And those whose task it is to spy out privily the doings of all men, and who spy out privily the doings of the highest in the land and the lowest (save only the doing of Hail, son of Sham, spy they not out privily, for he is virtuous, and upright, and holy, and cleanliving, and giveth advice unto God, therefore spy they not out privily his doings, even though they spy out privily the doings of all other men, yea of us as well as thee), these men say that they have seen thee entering in upon the dwelling of thy harlot, and they have seen other men entering in upon her dwelling also.'

Now when they had spoken thus, they fell silent, and the Elder of whom the dark things were said would have spoken, and would have wept, and rent his garments, and would fain have told them that these things were true. But they bade him fall silent again, and spoke again themselves after this wise.

'Lo, if all men speak these things, and all men write them, and thine epistles to thy harlot are seen in the market-place, and those who spy out privily upon the doings of all men have spied out privily upon thy doings and say also (like all other men) that these things are true, then canst thou not deny them, and they are true, and thou art an evil-doer, and art not worthy to sit at the right hand of Hail, son of Sham, who sitteth at the right hand of God, and giveth God advice. Therefore needest thou not speak, neither needest thou weep, nor beat thy breast, nor declare thy wrong-doing. But hearken instead unto us, and do as we bid thee. Lo, stand thou up upon the morrow in the market-place, and say in a loud voice that thou hast not lain with harlots, and that thou art not an evil-doer, and that thou wilt visit with the law all men who say that thou hast and art. And by the grace of God, and the grace of Hail, son of Sham, who sitteth upon his right hand, and giveth him advice, shall we all escape free from the burning. But before thou goest forth from us, say thou in a loud voice that thou hast not lain with harlots, and art not an evil-doer, that our consciences may be satisfied; and that afterwards we may blame thee with an open countenance.' But these last words spake they privily to themselves, and he heard them not.

And the Elder of whom the dark things were spoken did as they bade him, though his heart was heavy, and he knew he did wrong. But he could not choose. And it came to pass that all fell out as he feared, and worse even than he feared, and his name was a reproach for evermore in the ears of all men, and he vanished utterly from the earth, and it was as though he had never been. And the five Elders who had summoned him by night shook in their shoes, and looked with sideways glances upon each other, and feared lest the tale of their meeting with the Elder of whom the dark things were said should come to the ears of Hail, son of Sham, and he should question them, saying 'Now wherefore did ye not enquire further of the things ye heard, and put him upon the question, that ye might know whether he spoke truth or no?' And they feared this, for then would they have to beat their breasts, and rend their garments, and say that they had not enquired further lest they should find out the answers by so doing.

But they need not have feared, for Hail, son of Sham, questioned them not after this wise, neither questioned he them after any wise, though his heart was sore. And he went aside and took counsel with himself, and with his heart which was sore. And after he had taken counsel with himself he gave yet more advice unto God, yea, more than ten times the advice he had given unto God before, gave he then. And God took it not.

# 5 Three Songs

*What Have You Got?*

Take a man who's independent, and a lady
    like me
And a hill and a tree and a sky
Let an hour go by
Then returning to the spot
What have you got:
I'll tell you what

You've a man who's independent and a
    lady like me
And a sky and a tree and a hill
You can think what you will
Doesn't matter what you say
Love find a way
Love wins the day

I want a quiet oasis, one of those places
Make it not too cold or too hot
Where we know we're go'n' to do what
    we're prone to
Now we're getting bolder; Why not?

Take a man who's independent, and a lady
    like me
And a hill and a tree and a sky
Let an hour go by
Then returning to the spot
What have you got:
You got a lot of lovin', that's what

Who's to blame, takin' any man you name
A pair of sticks to rub to make a flame,
    all-a same
It'll all be simple free-and-easy, just as
    breezy as this
To tempt him with a kiss, you go down,

you prissy little miss
With an open bodice hopin' hard his
    mopin' eyes'll see the prize he's cravin'
He's gonna be savin' up a lot o' love for
    lavishin' over you

Blink it all, wink it all, think it all over
You take a man, a woman, and a mood
And the fun o' the game an' how you play,
    it changes with the man you got
Don Juan or nothin' doin': I'll try the lot:
    tot, hotshot, or momma's baby
Boy, what a joy they'll be

We'll make it
We'll take it on: if you've heard tell of a
    helluva
Lovin'up, that was me; that's how we'll be

Take a man who's independent and a lady
    like me
And a hill and a tree and a sky
Let an hour go by
Then returning to the spot
What have you got?
You got a lot of lovin': That's what.


*Roz* or *Why Didn't I Get To That Party*

I wasn't invited to come
To that little party chez vous
I'd have been delighted to come
If anybody'd asked me to
Was it a mistake? (Please don't trouble
    yourself)
Or on purpose, I wonder which
I didn't know if Roz was there
I wonder if she was, the little bitch

No, really, I wouldn't have come
Do let me assure you again
I honestly couldn't have come
I had to go on a date with Ken
You haven't a thing to be worried about
Let's forget it: oh what a bore
I wouldn't care it Roz was there
I wonder if she was: the little whore

Don't give it a thought:
In the middle of a muddle if you fiddle and
    you huddle
You can really diddle through
Makin' up your mind, you find, you do

Now it couldn't matter less to me if you
    were beggin'
Wouldn't I come, shouldn't I come,
    couldn't I come
I'd be there to tell you no
Go an' get up off your knees
It doesn't matter in the least

I hadn't intended to come
I felt no desire to go
Might have condescended to come
But only for an hour or so
I couldn't care less: don't be silly m'dear
Dead and buried, and that is that
I'm curious if Roz was there
I wonder if she was: the little rat
It's over and done, dead, gone, done, let's
    end this
Interminable tale of woe,
I've a little get-together, you must come:
    on the twentieth,
Seven-thirty, promise you'll be there,
With anyone you care to bring along

We'll open up a rare bottle o' wine
1937 you can only have a drop
No, there won't be many, hardly anybody
    comin'
And the strummin' of a low guitar

A bottle of wine, you, and a loaf of bread
Is all I require for my heart's desire

So say you'll be there
Hear y' knockin' at the gate
A little bit late
A quarter of an hour but you brought a
    little flower

Then I never know what should I say
It's ooh thank you and how-de-do

Fiddle about meet a friend o' mine-a name
    o' Dinah
Don't you know each other how'd you do
Glad you could come
And I'm glad you came alone

I got all tied up because
I thought you might have brought Roz
But let's not fight about Roz

Forget I brought it up, shut it up
Never wanna hear her name again

I know it's you an' me an' we can be a
    swingin' party together

Don't give it a thought:
In the middle of a muddle if you fiddle and
    you huddle
You can really diddle through
Makin' up you mind, you find you do

Now it couldn't matter less to me if you
    were beggin'
Wouldn't I come, shouldn't I come,
    couldn't I come
I'd be there to tell you no
Go an' get up off your knees
It doesn't matter in the least

I wasn't invited to come
To that little party chez vous
I'd have been delighted to come
If anybody'd asked to
Was it a mistake? (Please don't trouble
    yourself)
Or on purpose, I wonder which
I'm curious if Roz was was was there

I wonder if she was, the little bitch
I'm curious if Roz was there
I wonder if she was, the little . . .

    What I really want to know
    Is what has Rosalind got
    That I haven't got
    That she gets invited everywhere
      I don't.

## Mainly Physical

I think you're sweet as a rose, but that nose
The love inside me just grows, but that
    nose
You know I'm willing to bear what you
    wear
About the way that you stare I don't care
And your hair, oh I swear
I could forget about those, but that nose

I wake up in the morning and oh
Without any warning I know
That rather pensive, inner senses
Component of your anatomy
Will absolutely shatter me

I know I'd love you for years, but those ears
I'm never wholly at ease with those knees
I'm crazy for you, my sweet, but those feet
I close my eyes when we've met, to forget,
Shut 'em tight, dim the light
And slowly everything goes but that nose

Thinkin' of you baby
Cos I love you and I don't mean maybe
There's just an item or two that gets me
    low
If I recite 'em don't pack up and go
Cos I'm head over heel about
Dread what I feel about
Complainin'—you know I've got one
    continual fixation
Baby continuin'
All about this nose
With due consideration baby I suppose
I'm a fair disaster as to what the hell's
    cause of it
I can tell you how a little nose, which I
    suppose
Is just a nose, which only shows I'm a bit
    choosey over parts
Like heart and lips and hips and thighs and
    eyes and touch and such

I know I'd love you for years, but those
    ears.

All three songs by Steven Vinaver

I'm never wholly at ease with those knees
I'm always taken by storm by that form
I close my eyes, when we've met to forget,
Shut 'em tight, dim the light
I'm crazy for you
I do adore you
I think of you dear and everything glows
—But that nose!

# 6 Religion

*WHY?*    Robert Gillespie & Charles Lewsen

### A Consumer Guide to Religions

THIS WEEK 'Your Consumer Guide' presents its report on Religions. In seeking which was the best buy we first asked ourselves 'What should a good religion do?' And we decided that, ideally, it should offer a way of life, with strong reliable support under all circum-stances, culminating in happiness.

Of the dozens of products on the market we investigated the following six:

Judaism, the Roman Catholic Church, the Protestant Church, Islam, Buddhism and Communism.

We ruled out Hinduism. It embodies a caste system which we felt was alien to the British consumer. However, the Hindu does believe that animals have souls, every bit as good as human ones. In this sense it could be said that every Englishman is a Hindu at heart. But we felt that this did not outweigh the main objection.

We began by applying three basic tests:

(*a*)  What do you put into it?
(*b*)  What do you get out of it?
(*c*)  How much does it cost?

*Judaism*—This is the oldest religion we tested. Its small number of users (13 million) is deceptive, since many large and powerful subsidiaries derive from it. (*a*) What do you put into it? Belief in One Only God. Ten Dos and Don'ts. You must fast severely once a year; pray in Hebrew every morning and every evening; not eat pork or shellfish or dairy-produce with your meat; never prepare milk and meat in the same dishes; do no work between sunset on Friday and sunset on Saturday; And you must cut off the foreskins of your male children. (*b*) What do you get out of it? Membership of the oldest club in the world. A set of simple rules for solving your everyday living and thinking problems, backed by five thousand years of experience and a homely priesthood. Prayers and advice available are tailored to fit most consumer crises and can also be newly bespoke. 'YOU ARE ONE OF THE CHOSEN PEOPLE'—this gives confidence and we particularly liked the guarantee of Eternal Life through the Messiah or Saviour who will take responsibility for all your guilt—when he arrives. (*c*) What does it cost? In crockery alone the expense is fantastic plus the wages of a reliable Gentile to run the business between sunset on Friday and sunset on Saturday. Infertility is the only grounds for divorce. We did not try to obtain one.

We next tested the *Roman Catholic Church*. The vigorous new ideas of this splendid corporation were largely pioneered by the previous Group. But a superb sales organisation has enabled it to far outstrip the parent company with three hundred and forty million current users. Applying the tests we found: (*a*) What do you put into it? Belief in One Only God-head operating on a Troika basis. Belief that Jesus of Nazareth, Israel, living and working there two thousand years ago, is the Son of God. Belief in the Infallibility of Giovanni Battista Montini, now known as Paul the 6th, who was elected Head of the organisation in June. We must stress here that the idea that the Head (or Pope as he is called) claims infallibility in all matters is a fallacy. The Pope cannot tell you which television set is the best. His infallibility is strictly limited to matters of faith. He can only tell you which television programme you cannot watch. An interesting survival from classical prototypes is Virgin Birth. Most groups have dropped this labour-saving accessory but the testers found it refreshing and it gave no difficulty. We were pleased there were no white bulls or fornicating swans to contend with. Frequent mild fasting and constant attendance at services is required. (*b*) What do you get out of it? Principally the new CHRISTIANITY. This offers a policy of loving kindness, freewill and hope, evolved by a historically verified Messiah or Christ, in contrast to the vague promises and Eye-for-an-Eye outlook of Judaism. We noted that Jesus Christ has already undertaken personal responsibility for the consumer's misdemeanours. This gives extra support. And the confessional mechanism is standard; it operates as an added safety-factor to correct running mistakes, making Salvation almost foolproof. The rule here is 'DON'T'—but if you must, confess as soon as possible afterwards. We found this very useful. World-wide communications are maintained by using an international language—Latin. A comprehensive 'Life and Death' advisory service is available from a priesthood unencumbered by family ties. It provides high quality blessings, prayer, ritual and/or services, including the standard Mass for any occasion. A personal saint or intercessor with God is available to each consumer. A built-in Apostolic Succession ensures unique stability; and extremely high-quality by-products such as Madonna on the Rocks, Palestrina and Chartres Cathedral have attracted thousands of new consumers. With Roman Catholicism comes a guarantee that it is the *only true faith* and exclusive personal survival in heaven is assured. On the whole we found this product deeply satisfying. (*c*) What does it cost? A drawback—it is very expensive. During a visit to Head Office in Rome, a rosary or aid to prayer cost 100 lire; a small, votive candle 10 lire; devotional pictures 40 lire a time. We were charged 200 lire to see the catacombs; 300 lire to enter the Sistine Chapel (which is very dark); and a tour of the ante-rooms of St Peter's Basilica cost 300 lire in tips alone. We found it impossible to obtain a divorce.

*Protestantism* is a break-away of the Roman parent organisation. It arose in this country out of divorce proceedings in 1529. Two main brands are available: the Big Church of England or the Non-Conformist Economy Pack. (*a*) What do you put into it? Belief that the Queen should be Head of the Church. Belief that the Prime Minister should appoint the Archbishop of Canterbury. And belief in God and His Son Jesus Christ. (*b*) What do you get out of it? Independence. (*c*) How much does it cost? Surprisingly little. We found no difficulty in obtaining a divorce.

We next turned to *Islam* with 270 million users, founded thirteen hundred years ago. (*a*) What do you put into it? It is necessary to believe in One Only God and His Only True Prophet, Mohammed. Kneel down and pray five times a day facing Mecca. Begin services with the Lesser Ablution (Wudu) of face, hands and feet, the Greater Ablution (or Ghusl) being required only after Legal Pollution. Recite the Creed with full understanding once in your life. Go to Mecca once in your life. When you get there put on two seamless wrappers, do not shave, trim nails or anoint the head. Visit the sacred Mosque (Masjid alharam), kiss the Black Stone, go round the Ka'ba seven times, three times running, four times walking, visit the Maqam Ibrahim, climb Mount Sasfa, run from it to Mount Marwa seven times. Visit Mount Arafat. Hear a sermon. Go to Muzdalifa. Stay the night; throw stones at the three pillars in Mina on the Great Feast Day; offer sacrifice, and if convenient, visit the tomb of Mohammed. (b) What do you get out of it? Up to five wives. (c) How much does it cost? We had to buy a mat, and we found it very exhausting. We did not need to obtain a divorce.

*Buddhism*—the second oldest religion we tested is man-made, flexible and was designed by Buddha 2,522 years ago. It is available in two sizes: the Greater Vehicle (Mahayana) and Lesser Vehicle (Hyhayana). We concentrated on the better quality article—The Lesser Vehicle, with roughly 45 million users, since the other, though more popular, appears to be adulterated by additions of early Christianity and offers a similar service. (a) What do you put into it? Ten 'Don'ts' as follows:

1. Refrain from killing.
2. Refrain from stealing.
3. Refrain from unchastity.
4. Refrain from lying.
5. Refrain from intoxicants.
6. Refrain from solid food after midday.
7. Refrain from dancing music and theatrical representations.
8. Refrain from using garlands, perfumes and salves.
9. Refrain from using high and broad couches.
10. Refrain from accepting gold and silver.

(b) What do you get out of it? Nirvana—or, a sense of non-being. (c) What does it cost? Nothing. We did not try to get married.

We do not understand why *Communism* is on the market at all. It is very recent, mass-produced and its Chief Prophet appears to have no background in the industry at all. We were surprised at its enormous influence (900 million users) when we considered its inferior features. It replaces the standard Happiness-after-Death with promise of Comfort-during-Life which it hopes to achieve by sacrifice of the present generation for the future one, and of the individual for the group. We found this unpalatable and materialistic. Unchecked, we felt this could lead to a future life on earth of more or less endless pleasure, ending in something little short of general licence. Personal freedom, also, was severely curtailed by limiting the individual to do only work for which he was fitted. Finally the claim that this shoddy product must inevitably replace all others in the market we found rather shocking. As in the Church of England we found no difficulty in obtaining a divorce.

In conclusion we found that all the better religions offered perfect happiness in heaven as a reward for a good life. We decided to test these claims. Unfortunately we were unable to find anyone who would undertake this. Contact with the deceased also appeared to be difficult. We apologise for our failure to verify this important aspect of the product.

In choosing the best buy we rejected Islam as a cut-price form of Judaism. We admired Buddhism for its emphasis on personal effort with its resulting low cost. This product does not require belief in God but it is essential to follow the Maker's instructions closely which seriously interferes with normal living. A warning—the ban on killing includes all creatures, great and small. This can have distinct social disadvantages. But for the really desperate this product might be attempted, though we were unable to test the reincarnation process by which the desirable state of non-being is attained. The product does not travel well and thrives best in a warm climate.

Judaism we thought frankly unsafe. We recommend that unless you have it from birth you would do well to avoid this product.

If you can afford it, Roman Catholicism with its Continental Line plus international performance is well worth having. But we suggest that you should think carefully before deciding on it, as it is by no means trouble-free.

The attraction of the Church of England is its Democratic Spirit.

If you want Transubstantiation you can have Transubstantiation. If you don't want Transubstantiation, well then you don't have to have it. You can just walk down the road—into another church and not have it. If you want Mass you can have Mass. If you want Immaculate Conception you can have that too; but nobody will force you to have it if you don't want it. And the Church speaks to you in English. Of course, what will happen if we go into the Common Market, God only knows. But we think it'll be there— *speaking to you in English.*

And it's a jolly friendly faith. If you are one, there's no onus on you to make everyone else join. In fact no one need ever know. It doesn't interfere with essentials. And it's pretty fair on the whole. With some of these products—Roman Catholicism and Judaism for instance—you start guilty from the off. But with the C. of E., on the whole, you start pretty well innocent, and they've got to prove you're guilty.

You get eternal life—of course you get eternal life—but there's none of this toffee-nosed nonsense about the *only true faith* and the *chosen people* and so on.

All in all we think you get a jolly good little faith for a very moderate outlay and we have no hesitation in proclaiming it the Best Buy.

# 𝕳𝖞𝖒𝖓𝖘 𝕬𝖓𝖈𝖎𝖊𝖓𝖙   Caryl Brahms & Monica Furlong

HAVE YOU EVER been uneasy about the way the church infiltrates into other people's advertising copy. . . . Churchman's No. 1, Church's Shoes, Vicars Armstrong, Cannon Street, Deacons Bank, Curates Eggs. For that fuller flavour. But all this time, advertising has been quietly getting its own back on the Church. Particularly one sort of advertising.

Millions of Hymn Books are sold every year. All of them in use every Sunday . . . and all of them to the greater glory of God . . . and the motor industry.

> Hark the *Herald* angels sing
> Glory to the new-born king.

Hark the *Herald* angels sing. You can't tell us Leyland's didn't have a hand in that.

> The strife is o'er the battle done
> Now is the *Victor's triumph* won
> O let the song of praise be sung.   Alleluia.

*Victor. Triumph.* Both in the same line. You've got to hand it to them. What a jingle. Of course, like all advertising, our hymnals are apt to use lush language for the quality market. . . .

> What a rush of Alleluias
> Fills all the earth and sky.
> What ringing of a thousand harps
> Bespeaks the *Triumph* nigh.
> O day for which creation
> And all its tribes were made
> O joy for all its former woes
> A thousandfold repaid.

A thousandfold—that's Heaven, not the hire-purchase debt. But the best thing about this type of advertising is its feeling of moral fervour.

> Set up thy *Standard* Lord that they
> Who follow in the night
> May march with thee to smite the lies
> In Raiment clean and white.

In Raiment *clean* and *white*. Well, if you ask me Persil got together with *Standards* to achieve that one. But even the stateliest cars in the land are not entirely exempt from this kind of campaign.

> Yet with that car from Macedon
> The very car of Christ *Rolls* on.

Alfa!

> Of the Father's heart begotten
> E'er the world from chaos rose
> He is *Alpha*.

Zephyr!

> Sea and forest, frost and *Zephyr*.
> Day and night their Lord adore.

And there's even a hymn for St. George's Day (Hymns Ancient and Modern No. 758) which in three consecutive verses manages to bring in *Standard*, *Victor*, *Triumph*. And it isn't only cars either. Dr Beeching's a smart chap. Ever-zealous in the cause of British Railways—he's on to it too. . . .

> They climb'd the steep ascent of heaven
> Through peril, toil and pain,
> O God to us may grace be given
> To follow in the *train*.

Or 'It's warmer underground'. Well, I must be going now folks. Jesus wants me for a *Sunbeam*.

# Hymns Modern

## A NEW HYMN FOR THE BISHOP OF WOOLWICH     Sydney Carter

Your public image now, O Lord,
Is really out of date,
And we'd better get another
Before it is too late.

Glory Laud and Honour to
I really don't know who,
But keep on swinging the censer round
The way you used to do.

The old man with the whiskers
You see upon the wall,
You'd better look the other way,
He isn't there at all.

*Glory Laud and Honour to etc. . . .*

Half the things the Bible says
I don't believe are true,
And maybe I'm a bishop but
I think the same as you.

*Glory Laud and Honour to etc. . . .*

God without religion
Is what we want today:
You've got to tell the truth
Although they take your crook away.

Glory Laud and Honour to
I really don't know who,
But keep on swinging the censer round
The way you used to do.

## JERUSALEM     Caryl Brahms

And did those feet in ancient time
Walk upon Israel's mountains green,
And was the swarthy lamb of God
In Israel's pleasant pastures seen.
And did the countenance divine
Shine forth, hook-nosed, from Zion's hills,
And was Jerusalem builded there
In Tel Aviv's satanic mills.

Bring me the laws by Moses told
Bring me my arrows of desire
Bring me no spear, no gawds, no gold,
Bring me no chariot of fire.

I will not cease from mental fight
Until the world give him his due
Christ who was born in Bethlehem
A humble, poor and honest Jew.

## SUCCOUR     Lewis & Dobereiner

Oh God our help in Ages past,
Remember, we implore,
If we poor humans are the last
You'll have to make some more.

Teach thou our neighbours us to love
As we do love ourselves,
And make the fall-out up above
Fall out on someone else.

# TALKING WITH THE BISHOP     David Frost

*We print below the first and last in a series of conversations between David Frost and the recently appointed Bishop of Chiswick, The Rev. Martyn Brackwell.*

FROST: Good afternoon, my Lord.

CHISWICK: Good afternoon, young man.

FROST: I see you're not wearing your bright red . . .

CHISWICK: No, I'm not.

F: Do you still feel, Dr Brackwell, as you did when you said: 'Anyone—and there are such people—who earns more than £40 a week should keep £5 and throw the rest away, or forfeit the name of "Christian" '?

C: I doubt very much if I ever . . . Oh, you've got it there. What I meant was, after tax had been deducted. That's it. After tax had been deducted.

F: I see here that you argued a very good case in one of our more enterprising newspapers for the disestablishment of . . .

C: Some time ago, I think.

F: January 1960.

C: Ah . . . things have changed since then.

F: When in Rome . . .

C: Yes. No, no.

F: You also wrote a pungent series in which you most ably attacked the Church on three main counts. First, the clergy; second, the congregations; and third, the churches themselves. I suppose that now . . .

C: Whatever happens, I don't want to give anyone the impression that I'm merely a critic of the way the Church is run. That's the last thing I want to do. You've only mentioned one side . . .

F: You feel that there is another side?

C: Rather.

F: What exactly?

C: Well, as I travel about the Underground, I can't help noticing how much better the church notice-boards are being kept. And I think that's a good sign, don't you?

F: Yes.

C: And you'd hardly compare the measly little collection plates we used, say, ten years ago, with the ones we use today.

F: I see that you said here: 'If anyone was ever silly enough to make me a bishop, and there were so-called vicars in my diocese who were getting hold of less than thirty new members per annum, I'd get rid of them—and fast.' At Chiswick, you'll be able . . .

C: If I remember rightly, that was a quick sally at a naval and military dinner near Devon. You must surely realise by now that words cannot . . .

F: I got it from your church magazine.

C: Oh yes, that's right. My warden was the editor, and he used to hunt out little quotes that he thought would embarrass me. He was a great fellow. Ha, ha. A great fellow.

F: This particular one is actually from a reprint of one of your sermons. It's called 'What shall we do with the cathedrals? No. 2.' You obviously . . .

C: Yes, but of course it's all got to be taken in its context. You can't just pick out odd bits, and hope to . . . Oh no, don't trouble to find it now. You haven't got much longer.

F: One thing I have always admired you for, Dr Brackwell, is your fearless political courage.

C: I'm not sure that I quite . . .

F: I shall never forget hearing you say, 'No one can be both a Christian and a Conservative.'

C: 'At the same time.' You forgot that. It may not have been down on your little piece of paper, but you forgot it. 'At the same time'—that's the important phrase. I mean you can't vote for Lord Home and burn incense in the same breath, can you? You've got to look back and see how the words can best be interpreted—as I'm trying to do now. But I mustn't keep you any longer—you've got a wife and family to think of, Mr Frost.

F: No, I haven't.

C: All the more reason why you should hurry. Good afternoon, Mr Frost.

F: Good afternoon.

## TRAVELOGUE    Keith Waterhouse & Willis Hall

*And there was traffic, and the A23 from London to Brighton was solid with it. From Crawley to Pease Pottage, from Handcross to Cuckfield, even on the Gatwick Clearway there was a honking and a hooting and a sounding of horns.*

You know, what is the significance of Easter? There is a very simple answer to that. A friend of mine, a very simple chap really, said to me: 'You know, Warden, I look forward to Easter because I can take the wife and kiddies for a drive down the Exeter By-pass.'

'I look forward to Easter.' But do you know, did that chap really appreciate what Easter is all about?

Officially, of course it's the second festival in the traffic warden's calendar. The first is Christmas, when we decorate the West End to draw the traffic and then ban all the cars from parking, and the second is Easter. But there is really much more to it than that.

Easter, quite simply, is the time when we think about sin. And that sin is the sin of parking in unauthorised places. Oh yes, it is a sin. I know that in these modern enlightened times it's fashionable to talk about technical offences and minor infringements. There was a time, not so very long ago, when I would talk like that. And then one day I happened to see a Bentley parked in a mews—quite harmlessly, some people would have said. But it suddenly came to me that the motor car is the symbol of all that is wrong with the world— the pride and the lust and the envy and the possessiveness. Parking is a sin. Our leader, Mr Marples, believes it is a sin, and he believes quite simply that we must be punished for our trespasses.

So, at this Easter-time, very simply, your car will be chivvied and hounded off the road. The luckier ones among us will have their cars towed away and will expiate their sins here on earth. The less fortunate will sit in traffic jams ruminating on what they have done, cast into limbo or purgatory if you like, on an M1 lay-by.

*In Kingston-upon-Thames, and in Morden, and along the road that some folks say leads to Eastbourne, there was a pulling of chokes and a grinding of gears. And there were traffic jams outside the empty churches in Lewes and Haywards Heath and Burgess Hill. Forgive them, Lord, for they know not where they are going.*

# 7 People

*NEW INSTANT WILSON*    David Frost & Christopher Booker

*A supplementary advertising campaign on behalf of the Labour Party.*

I cannot tell new Instant Wilson from old pipe-smoking Attlee.
*P.S.* I can't tell new Instant Wilson from old stab-in-the-back Wilson.

**I was a floating Voter until they discovered Wilson—now I'm sunk.**

**Forget those nasty scruples
—with WILSON.**

**Only WILSON
gets right under the skin.**

HUGHIE: Now we have the two commodities here and I'm going to ask Milly here, who's blindfolded at the moment, if she can tell the difference.

The difference between the one that's only been washed white once—and the one that's been whitewashed consistently for the past few months.

MILLY: Well, I think it's the one on the left.

HUGHIE: I see, and would you like to know which that is?

MILLY: Oh yes, I'd love to.

HUGHIE: Well, would you just take that card . . .

MILLY: OOOOOOOOOOOH. It's Wilson!

HUGHIE: It certainly is, Milly—and why did you choose WILSON?

MILLY: Well, I thought that other one was probably cleaner . . . but it wasn't so Bright. Whereas the Wilson made me think straightaway of shining white collars. And I hear the Wilson's the one with the mystery ingredient.

HUGHIE: Yes. Ladies and gentlemen, Milly chose Wilson—the product which wasn't TIED. To anything. *For remember 144 out of every 249 Labour MP's prefer WILSON.*

At 25 I was only a don—what did I need with a policy?

At 35 I was in the Cabinet—I was sure that a policy would only tie me down.

At 45 I began to worry about the future Labour offered—but I knew that a policy would be the biggest disadvantage of all.

But today at 46, at last I can afford a policy. Any ideas?

Is there a Leak in Your Bank Rate? October 1957; writes HW of Huyton, Lancs.

'I have *prima facie* evidence of a leak'.

But only three months later HW wrote to us again:

'We never said there was a leak'.

Yes, be like HW—if you have a leak, puff on your pipes and plumb the depths.

You'll wonder where the George Brown went When Harold forms his Government.

# Wilson causes Labour-blur.

*Darling, please bath George Brown.*

*You'll look a little lovelier each day With fabulous Douglas Jay*

Don't think of Wilson as merely a commodity—you don't use Wilson. Wilson uses YOU.

## MOTHERS' DAY   David Nathan & Dennis Potter

### WHAT IS A MUM?

A Mum lives with a Dad and 2·4 children in a rented house where the neighbours notice her washing on the line. A Mum relies upon secret ingredients and instant cake-mixes. She has kids with dirty teeth who regularly shout 'Don't forget the Fruit Gums, Mum'.

A Mum is full of faith. She thinks every wash-day is a miracle. And since she adds the extra egg to everything except the bacon, she is probably constipated as well.

A Mum lives in a warm house. If she's been conned into having oil-fired central heating, she opens the door for the postman wearing a baby-doll nightdress. Mrs 1970 is a tart.

But a Mum is very unpopular with teenagers. She keeps interrupting their orgies with steaming mugs of cocoa.

A Mum goes to Butlins and worries about dandruff. And sometimes the poor soul feels run-down and lacking in energy. Then, she's so confused that if she gets a fever of a 100 she thinks she is feeling one degree under. I know why. Her old man bashes her about because every time he comes home tired and famished she tells him that a little cube of beef stock is a real man's meal.

A Mum is a right nit. She keeps tea fit only for chimpanzees. She gives her kids tins of pork luncheon meat and her dog tons of real chunky butcher's meat. She buys disinfectants that make her clean round the bend.

That's why a Mum doesn't think. Her hands are as soft as her head. She is so flaming ignorant that she can't tell Stork from butter . . . or even Stork from margarine. She thinks a Free Gift is something she doesn't have to pay for.

A Mum, in short, is a snob who buys plastic flowers and floor polish containing real lavender. She solves emotional problems with Horlicks and on Mother's Day this idle, ignorant, tasteless and irresponsible lump of girdle-encased margarine fat has the cheek to turn round and expect US to buy *her* a bleeding present!

## CONFESSION    John Braine

*Security cases like Houghton, Lonsdale, Peter and Helen Kroger, and Profumo leave an awkward question in the public mind. . . .*

Heterosexuality is an ugly word. Until recently it skulked in the obscurity of medical text books. Now, one hears it everywhere. Let us be explicit and fearless about its meaning, then. *Hetero*, as one might expect, is derived from a foreign language, and means 'opposite'. Therefore, a heterosexual man is sexually attracted only to women and vice-versa.

There are few outward signs by which a heterosexual reveals himself, though authorities on the subject claim that a heterosexual will sooner or later give himself away—if only by his clumsiness and coldness, and crashing insensitivity. A heterosexual walks—or rather clumps in hobnailed boots and belted mac—alone. Not for him the joys of true comradeship; his energies are all spent in the pursuit of women. There is nothing he longs for more, than a night out with the boys, but a night out with the boys—in the truest, deepest sense— is precisely what he can never enjoy. He is too busy making passes at the barmaid.

What is being done about this problem? Very little. The prevalent official attitude is simply to make heterosexuality as difficult as possible, to scoop it under the carpet.

How do I know all this?

I am a heterosexual.

It began early with me, at my public school. I won't say which one . . . I have dishonoured it enough already. I was fourteen years old, apparently a happy, wholesome normal lad, making friendships which would stand me in good stead for the rest of my life, when suddenly I realised that I didn't feel as I should towards the Captain of the Eleven. I couldn't disguise my growing conviction that he was a big, fat, boring slob. The padre, the housemaster, the housemaster's wife, did their level best to help, but I left school under a cloud.

I became an up-and-coming young executive. My field was corsets. I was good at my job, then one afternoon, I found it necessary to take a client to a strip club. I was watching a young lady in a G-string wrestling with a stuffed snake, when, to my horror, I discovered that I violently desired her. I tried to believe that it was something I had eaten. I tried to behave normally, and only looked at the audience. But it was no use. I enjoyed looking at naked women.

Of course, my work began to suffer. I lost my job. Now, I am a doorman at the strip club which was the cause of my downfall. I am not actively unhappy, and sometimes the young ladies let me take them home, but it's a strange twilight world I live in. I have fallen farther than most, because I had farther to fall.

Mine is a sad story, but heterosexuals do not cry. I am not a criminal. Before you condemn me out of hand, try and see me as I am, a lost and lonely soul, with perhaps, a more than passing resemblance to—dare I say it—yourselves.

## DE GAULLE

### Peter Lewis & Peter Dobereiner

GENERAL DE GAULLE first came to our notice as leader of the Free French under the emblem of the cross of Lorraine—or to be strictly accurate the double cross of Lorraine. Sir Winston Churchill, who served in a minor capacity on the general's staff when De Gaulle was winning the war, once remarked that it was the heaviest cross he had to bear.

His attitude to the Common Market was made clear in 1947 when he said of European union: 'It has always been impossible to organise such a Europe before. Always in the past one nation has sought to dominate the others. For the first time such conditions no longer exist.'

De Gaulle has completely identified France with himself referring to my army, my bomb, my Mediterranean, my France, my Europe and even at times has been known to exclaim 'Mon Dieu!'

What has he got against Britain? He has made this quite clear. He has said: 'If anyone says Britain is an island everyone is lost in amazement. But this is an evident fact.' He's got something against islands, you see, ever since he read about Elba and St Helena. But we must clear up one misconception about his attitude. Even though we are an island he is quite prepared to go on letting the Imperial War Graves Commission into France to look after the British army cemeteries.

To give him his due he has many fine qualities, not least a complete lack of fear for his personal safety. His ministers may worry themselves sick every time he takes a plane trip. Not De Gaulle. He knows that if the plane does come down in the sea he can always get out and walk.

# THE PRESIDENT OF FRANCE   Peter Shaffer

IT IS 1990. *The President of France was this morning elected Supreme Chief Spokesman of the European Community. This afternoon this grand old veteran made his speech of acceptance before the Council of Europe.*

(THE PRESIDENT IS A TREMENDOUS OLD MAN. IN HIS DELIVERY AND GESTURES HE IS ELABORATE, THEATRICAL, BUT FORCEFUL. HE STANDS AT A LECTERN.)

Friends! Europeans! Countrymen! The result of this election has filled me with profound satisfaction. You have called me to this great office of Chief Spokesman for Europe. How tremendous! How unique! And how fitting! Yes!—how fitting! This is no time, gentlemen, for false modesty, for public demonstrations of humility, or confessions of unworthiness. Because I am far from being unworthy. In fact, I am very worthy indeed! Some of the humbler among you may ask: 'How dare he say this?' I will tell you. Firstly, because I am a successful soldier. A general. This means that I have met the supreme test of personal integrity. I have been prepared to slaughter millions of my fellows to achieve military advantage. To give orders willingly, if necessary, which could burn them to death, blind them for life, or leave them castrated and hung up over barbed wire after a bayonet charge. This means that I care nothing for individuals. I care only for ideals! How magnificent! Europe has always worshipped her soldier-idealists, provided they are violent enough, and withdrawn enough from common sympathy. Even the sentimental English grovel at the feet of their Wellingtons, their Haigs, their Montgomerys. The Churches of Europe have always received their dead bodies with honour, and enshrined their savagery in gigantic tombs which effectively blot out the light from stained glass windows proclaiming the verbal virtues of gentleness and mercy. In every parish church there is a roll of honour of those who died dropping bombs on their fellow men.

St Paul's Cathedral in London boasts a high altar dedicated to the memories of men whose sole distinction is that they practised murder. And this is as it should be. Under all that Protestant cant, Europe still worships force. It was only when Britain has surrendered every vestige of Might that she fell to whining about Right (*Laughter*).

Secondly, I am worthy to lead you because I am a Frenchman. My ancestors are Charlemagne; the Sun King, Louis; Bonaparte. In their bodies were centred the aspirations, the spiritual dreams of a continent which is now, today, what it has always been; the only civilised land-mass on earth (*Applause*). What is Africa? A farmyard of black animals—fetish and famine! The throats that there cry obedience to Parliamentary law, still thirst to drink human blood! (*Applause*). Their Cabinet Ministers are nothing but witchdoctors in altered dress! (*Laughter*). The judge's wig, the policeman's helmet—these are nothing to them but new objects of primitive magic! On my authority we abandoned Africa—and how wise I was! Only so could we keep ourselves pure, French and Catholic (*Applause*).

What is Asia? A wilderness of indistinguishable peasants, sunk alike in the same desperate anonymity—which they assure us is the chief blessing Communism can confer! (*Applause*). Asia has nothing to offer the world but her poverty and her pathetic concern with imitation. Just as America has nothing to offer it but her wealth, and her neurotic concern with invention. America spends her days wondering what maturity can be like. Asia has long ago forgotten (*Laughter*). As for Australia. Well (*Redoubled laughter*).

There is, of course, no country in the British Commonwealth that is even on nodding terms with civilisation. The most they can claim is the Pioneering Spirit. And what is that but a spirit of demolition masquerading as one of construction? Europe is the only vital continent. And France—I repeat it—is Europe.

Well? Do I lie? What are all of you compared with me? Babies! You, little Holland, little Belgium! Born in 1830. You, Italy—1860. You, Germany—1870. Babies, every one of you. I was here in AD 1000! England alone can rival me in antiquity—and England has never been Europe. She has always hated us! You well know this is true, my children. And especially me. Especially me!

God knows it's true! Crecy, Agincourt, Blenheim, Trafalgar, Waterloo! Acts of sheer unprovoked hatred, all of them! What was her famous Entente Cordiale? The scared smile of an old lady, terrified of death, hoping to appease God for centuries of hostility against his Chosen People. But God is not deceived, my dear children. He has blighted the British Empire! He has given leadership into the hands of France! The Community of Europe, led by me, is His State established on earth: Civitas Dei! In olden times we called it the Holy Roman Empire. Now it is the Holy French Empire! (*Here the President produces the Crown of France.*)

Look, my babies. With this sacred object, Napoleon crowned himself King of France. Since then it has increased in holiness. It is electric with the will of all true Europeans to keep the flame of virtue burning in the otherwise empty lamp of the terrestrial world. (*Raising the crown.*) With God's blessing, I crown myself King of Europe! Seigneur of Brussels! Suzerain of the Hague! Feudal Overlord of West Berlin! Warden in Chief of the Vatican! Long live French Catholic Europe! (*Cheers.*)

And may God in His wisdom give fury to our missiles and power to our bomb, that we may protect forever this final revelation of His divine will on earth! (*The President then crowns himself amidst acclamation. The Marseillaise.*)

## TIME AND J. B. PRIESTLEY    Keith Waterhouse & Willis Hall

J. B. PRIESTLEY is experimenting with Time—again. In 'Monitor' he explained to a mystified Huw Wheldon about the new book—yet another new book—he is writing about Time. We know, because he has told us repeatedly, what J. B. Priestley thinks about Time. But what does Time think about J. B. Priestley?

INTERVIEWER: Father Time, is it true that you're working on a theory that's going to reveal to us the secret of the Universe?

FATHER TIME: (*who smokes a pipe and looks suspiciously like J. B. Priestley*). Well, I'm no expert. I'm not a physicist and I'm not a mathematician and, in the purest sense, I suppose you could say I'm not even a historian, but I have an inkling—it's no more than an inkling—that it's all got something to do with J. B. Priestley.

INTERVIEWER: That really is an extraordinary theory.

FATHER TIME: It is, isn't it? Mark you, in plain man's language I think it'd be fair to add that I don't know what I'm talking about.

INTERVIEWER: Allowing that, could you expand on your ideas at all?

FATHER TIME: Well, I could describe about ninety to a hundred dreams I've been having recently. . . .

INTERVIEWER: Perhaps, just one.

FATHER TIME: I dreamed that I was in a hall. A vast hall. And this hall had seats and curtains and a stage and usherettes and programme sellers, and I judged that I must be in a theatre of some kind. And they were doing in rapid succession all sorts of plays such as 'When We Are Married' and 'An Inspector Calls' and 'The Linden Tree' and there was wild applause. Then J. B. Priestley himself appeared and said, 'Now I am going to talk about Time'. And, miraculously, the theatre emptied.

INTERVIEWER: How do you interpret this extraordinary vision?

FATHER TIME: I believe that everything we do, everything we are, everything we think and everything we believe is in some mysterious way connected with J. B. Priestley.

INTERVIEWER: Have you any actual proof of this?

FATHER TIME: None whatsoever. I'm hoping, however, that people will come forward and give me examples for my book. I'm sure that many people—publishers, for example, theatre managers—must have had strange dreams or, indeed, nightmares, in which J. B. Priestley has appeared, talking about Time.

INTERVIEWER: Could you explain your theory in layman's language?

FATHER TIME: I couldn't explain it in anything else. Somebody—Einstein probably, I'd have to look it up—told us that Time is in the shape of a figure eight, so that no matter what point we start from we must in-ex-orably arrive back at the same point.

INTERVIEWER: That's beyond me, I'm afraid.

FATHER TIME: It's beyond me as well, but the point I'm trying to make is that J. B. Priestley, too, is in the shape of a figure eight, and that he's going to go on and on arriving at the same point and writing the same bloody book.

INTERVIEWER: What do you think is behind this extraordinary phenomenon?

FATHER TIME: I think there's a very simple explanation. J. B. Priestley is a brilliant writer who, some years ago, started experimenting with Time. And ever since then, Time has been experimenting with J. B. Priestley.

## 1945

If that fellah Attlee gets in we will have the Gestapo here. Churchill says so.

Quite right, quite right.

## 1946

See what Earl Winterton says: 'Mr Attlee seems unable to exert any influence upon ominous world events.'

That's very true, very true.

## 1947

See what Crookshank says today: 'We have always thought there was no Prime Minister and now we know it.'

I think Lord Balfour puts it better: 'Mr Attlee's flickering candle of hesitancy and half measure.'

That's very, very good.

## 1948

Fellah here says that if Mr Attlee were to resign his office, if this Parliament could be dissolved, such a sigh of relief would go up all over the world as would astonish us.

Who said that?

Fellah called Harold Macmillan.

Whatever happened to him?

Dunno.

### 1949

Heard the latest Attlee story? An empty taxi drew up outside the House of Commons and Mr Attlee got out. Ha ha!

Ha ha! Good as that description of him—a sheep in sheep's clothing.

See how Bracken described his speech: 'The pipings and bleatings of an asthmatic rabbit.' I like that. Yes, I like it.

### 1950

I think Lord Birkenhead puts it very well when he says that Mr Attlee is in no whit abashed by all his previous follies and miscalculations.

No whit, no whit.

### 1951

Rab says he appears to be walking in his sleep.

Don't know how the fellah got back in power.

He lulled us. That chap Christopher Hollis says so.

He says Attlee has been lulling his party as well as the nation.

Lulling, lulling, very good.

### 1962

A great Englishman!

Who?

Attlee of course. Christopher Hollis says so. He says Attlee is not only one of the great English Prime Ministers but also one of the great English characters.

He is?

Course he is. Hollis has written a piece about him in the *Observer*. (*Reads.*) 'He smokes a pipe as we all do. He follows county cricket scores as we all do.'

But I don't quite see . . . what happened?

Don't be an idiot. Nothing happened of course. But the fellah had an 80th birthday last week.

I see, I see. How silly of me. Great Englishman. Very, very great.

One of the best, old boy. One of the best.

# 'INTERNAL COMBUSTION'   David Nobbs

REVIEWING THE BRITISH film comedy 'The Fast Lady'—based on the idea that cars are funny—Penelope Gilliatt said in the *Observer* that English films seem to use cars instead of sex in a particularly British sort of symbolism that was worth exploring. . . .

*I'm a nice car.*
Yes. How many cylinders have you got?
*Two.*
Good. And you're only eighteen horsepower.
*No. Please. Don't start.*
What's wrong?
*It's been so nice. Don't spoil everything.*
Women!
*I'm sorry. I can't help it.*
Here. Have a sump oil.
*You just want to get me tanked up, don't you? And then before I know where I am you'll be obtaining the power for automatic clutch operation by making use of the partial vacuum in the engine inlet manifold.*
I just want to take you for a drive.
*I'm sorry. But a girl's got so much to lose. She's never the same once she's been decarbonised.*
Well, I'm off, then.
*No, don't. Well, just a little ride. But not fast.*
(HE SETS OFF) *Be gentle with me. I haven't got shock absorbers.*
Change gear (SHE CHANGES GEAR) Horn. (SHE BLOWS THE HORN)
*I like that.* (SHE BLOWS THE HORN AGAIN)
Double bend.
*Do it again.*
We'd be in the hedge. (PAUSE) Let's double de-clutch, Mildred.
*No—I—please. Be patient with me. I may later.*
That's right. Keep yourself in a state of independent front-wheel suspension—a disadvantage of which is that the unsprung weight of the heavy beam axle is inconsistent with good road-holding.
*I loved the way you said that.*
You did? You know you wouldn't look bad if you used a bit more anti-freeze.
*Do another double bend.*
It's kinky.
*It's not. I like other things.*
Such as?
*I don't like to say it.*
Go on.

(COYLY) *I like it when you move the gear lever and close the switch, thus energising the solenoid and causing the left hand side of the piston to be exposed to the partial vacuum in the reservoir.*
You've been driven by other men.
*You've driven other women.*
It's not the same thing.
*Why are you stopping? I'm not going in a lay-by with a strange man.*
I'm not stopping.
*What are you doing?*
Reversing.
*Pervert.*

# EDGAR LUSTGARTEN    Keith Waterhouse & Willis Hall

*For many years Mr Edgar Lustgarten has regaled the readers of the evening papers with his recon-
structions of famous trials. The Women in the Case, the Man in the Case, the Judge in the Case, the
Prosecuting Counsel in the Case and the Defending Counsel in the Case are all meat and drink to Mr
Lustgarten.*

*In the same week that a new Lustgarten series began, a Mr Jack Merricks appeared before the
disciplinary committee of the Potato Marketing Board and there were some ugly outbursts when Mr
Merricks called the committee 'a Fred Karno court which was good enough for the Crazy Gang'.*

*Here is high drama indeed, and we've been wondering why Mr Lustgarten doesn't make the hearings
of the Potato Marketing Board the subject of his next series. With our compliments, the first instal-
ment of the Potato in the Case.*

. . . Of all the witnesses who have pointed the bold finger of truth in the dramatic
chambers of justice, none has been more decisive or more damning than Mother Nature
herself.

It was Nature whose rains uncovered the Boston Torso which sent John William
Mathieson to the gallows. It was Nature whose winds blew through the kale fields of
Wiltshire to reveal the charred glove that hanged Thomas James Potter. And it was
Mother Nature, dropping the microscopic spore of a parasitic fungus into the scales of
justice, that brought retribution on the head of Charles Henry Proudfoot.

The case against Proudfoot was an astonishing one. It was that in 1959 he failed to
make a return on an acre of King Edward potatoes planted in a remote field in Lincolnshire. Did any of us who saw the swaggering farmer, as he faced the accusers on that fate-
ful afternoon, suspect that beneath the blustering exterior beat a craven and guilty heart?
If not, we were soon to know, and know in no undramatic fashion.

'You're a pack of old women!' shouts the arrogant potato grower. But soon his very
confidence is to lead him irrevocably into the jaws of justice.

Sir Peter Farthingale opens the case with the dry, salty wit that has made him loved
and feared within the Potato Marketing Board.

'Mr Proudfoot, did you make these returns?'

*Did you make these returns.* An innocent enough question on the face of it. And Charles
Henry Proudfoot, consumed with his own self-importance, falls immediately into the
trap.

'Why should I?' he snaps.

*Why should I.* Already the net is closing in. Too late the cocky rascal sees where his
arrogance is leading him. Smoothly, and with dangerous knife-edge rhetoric, Sir Peter
drives home his point.

'So you admit that you did not make these returns.'

A deathly silence. The knuckles of Proudfoot's hands show white as he grips the dock.
But his cockiness is not yet spent.

'I just said so, didn't I?'

Oh, foolish Proudfoot! The net of justice is drawing in and it is your own hands that
pull home this bitter haul! Sir Peter, now disconcertingly, dangerously calm, puts an
apparently routine question.

'So we may take it that these returns were never made.'

It is the chink in Proudfoot's armour. 'Oh, shut up!' he cries, goaded beyond reason. Sir Peter, suave and silky, waits for the outburst to finish.

'Is it not a fact that your entire potato crop was wiped out by late blight in 1959?'

A loaded question. Does Charles Henry Proudfoot see at least the trap that yawns before him?

He licks his lips. Probing, pressing, prying, Sir Peter remorselessly repeats the question. 'Was your potato crop wiped out by late blight?'

'Of course it was, you silly old faggot! That's why I didn't make a return.'

The high drama is over. The blood drains from Proudfoot's face and he realises where his over-confidence has got him. In the deathly silence, the chairman of the Disciplinary Committee of the Potato Marketing Board addresses him. 'Mr Proudfoot, it has been established that you did not make these returns and you must pay a penalty of £75.'

The broken farmer is helped out of court. A woman in the public benches quietly weeps. Justice has been done. But how many realise on how thin a thread the sword of retribution hung—that had not Mother Nature chosen to send late blight to a remote potato field in Lincolnshire, Charles Henry Proudfoot might still be nursing his guilty secret?

## THE MAN WHO'S NOT FROM COOK'S    David Nobbs

TRAVEL THE POLYTHENE way this year. Polythene—the all-in tours, the package tours that are really a package. Yes, your luxury dormocoach is entirely covered in a huge polythene bag that gives you complete protection from absolutely everything. Except your fellow-travellers that is, and to give you complete protection from them, too, there's a person-sized polythene bag for each person. So, provided you're person-sized, travel Polythene this year. £400 for 14 days and no time wasted in stopping or starting. You just trundle along day and night, encased in your wondrous slumberbag, at 40 m.p.h. You cover 960 miles a day—that's 13,000 miles in all. Indeed you can, in a sense, do 26,000—lots of our clients discover that they've gone on one tour and their luggage on another. So travel the Polythene way. Each dormocoach has a narrow strip along both sides filled with climate—British climate. Just pull the nozzle of the person-sized bag and you can luxuriate in intermittent drizzle.

It's in the bag with Polythene, the all-in tour.

Don't like the scenery abroad? Lots of flat bits and then all those Alps bunched together in one corner? No trouble with Polythene. As you wind across the Stelvio pass, the snow glinting on the sharp peaks of the Dolomites, the sky blue above you and the valley beneath, Polythene scenic consultants play you a film of reclaimed land in the Soke of Peterborough.

Best of all, perhaps, are the Polycards. The Polycard girl will fill in your name—Polythene Traveller 3764 or whatever it is—and the rest's already done with the delightful message: 'Having a wonderful time. Food very nice. Coach nice. Weather nice. Scenery nice. Nice nice.'

That's Polythene, the all-in tour. The journey's all-in. The food's all-in. And by the end the customers are all-in.

## *AN APPEAL TO DR BEECHING*   Caryl Brahms

THE BRANCH LINES under the threat of Dr Beeching's axe occupied the attention of rural travellers and train-spotters throughout the year. One letter read:

'I travelled on the last passenger train last summer and bought the last dog ticket from Watermoor to South Cerney, and all the railway men were in best boots and with smart buttons.'

*Withington Halt, Chedworth Halt, Alvercot,*
*Chelmscott, Longford and Lechlade,*
*Bourton-on-the-Water, Stow-on-the-Wold,*
*Brize Norton . . . Norton . . . Norton . . . Norton*
*Burbage and Bourne.*

Spare, Woodman, spare the Beeching branch from Haywards Heath to Horstead Keynes,
Spare, too, the eleven fifty-four to trundle down its iron lanes.
Be merciful to railway stations, to Lewes, all change here for Glynde,
Where we have waited for relations on platforms open to the wind.
People in fields at Chipping Norton, how will they know the time of day
Should the twelve-twenty cease to run eight minutes late down Didcot way?

And oh the anguish at the deep heart's core,
The milk train does not stop here any more!

Good Doctor, have you never dawdled where the down train should have been,
Breathed in the unforgettable, unforgotten station smell, part dust, part kerosene?
Let your degree, your Ph.D. earned in the field of electronics,
Prove to the world man's proper study is viable Railway Economics.

*Walsingham, Snettisham,*
*Halesworth and Beccles . . . Beccles . . . Beccles . . .*
*Burbage and Bourne.*

Old engines with their primal anger gone,
Their fire and fury rusted quite away,
No longer chuffing into Platform One,
Butchered to make a scrapyard holiday.

Don't think they will not take it hard at Hatch
Thorn Falcon, Donyatt, Chard, their summary dispatch.

Back to the pack old dragons! No one cares
For galleons, balloons, stage coaches, sedan chairs.

And oh the silence when the stations die,
In Tewkesbury, Ripple, Brill, Fairford and Ardingly.

*Eastleigh, Romsey, Andover and Savernake,*
*Bowers Gifford, Benfleet, Laindon, Leigh,*
*Wickford, Shoebury, Swaffham and Saxmundham,*
*Stamford-le-hope . . . hope . . . hope . . . hope*
*Burbage and Bourne.*

And oh the silence when the stations die
In Tewkesbury, Ripple, Brill, Fairford and Ardingly.

## THESE ARE THE THINGS

*MR DAVID HICKS, the interior decorator, gave an interview last October. Asked what he hoped to achieve as a designer Mr Hicks replied modestly, 'I want to design curtains and upholstery, materials, supermarkets, outside television aerials, coathangers, cereal packets, dustbins ... and a list as long as your arm.'*

*Mr Hicks went on, 'Many of these things I care deeply about, and all of them could and must be re-designed.'*

The things I care about are cereal packets,
Delicious dustbins in amusing jackets,
Door handles and
Silver grandstands,
These are the things about which I care.

A racing car and then the place to park it:
A lemon jelly and a super-market;
These could and must
Be redesigned.
These are the things about which I mind.

Strange how my fingers itch. To get at a cricket
    pitch,
And something deep inside me says why keep
    Britain tidy.
Let's make it beautiful,
For us to share.

## Caryl Brahms & Ned Sherrin

I've got new thoughts for speedboats and coat-
   hangers,
I've always thought mash would look well with
   bangers.
That may be new,
But I'll break through,
These are the things about which I care.

All things bright and beautiful,
China and dress fabrics,
Watches, toys and hearses,
Designed by David Hicks.

Farm buildings, fences, aeroplane interiors,
Both for my equals and my social inferiors,
A rocket base,
A rocking chair,
These are the things about which I care
And care for deeply
And charge for steeply
These are the things about which I care.

# CANON COLLINS     David Nathan & Dennis Potter

*Two very young men and a girl are discussing Canon Collins. One man, A, is not sure about him, the other, B, is aggressively against, the girl, hair bunned back, spectacled, is violently pro-Collins.*

A: Now that we have set up the National Campaign for the Abolition of Bombs, Bishops, Hanging, Drunken Drivers and South African imports, the NCABBHSI—or NAT-PROTEST—for short—all that we need is someone to serve on the committee who is nationally known, highly respected. With good feet . . .

B: Ay, there'll be plenty of marching.

A: And an ability to write appealing letters.

GIRL: He should have some sex-appeal as well. Not that it bothers me, of course. But we do want the popular press to take some notice of us. I suggest Canon Collins.

B: What, him again? Don't you think people are a bit tired of him?

GIRL: Perhaps, but surely we have to balance that against the magic of his name and the strength of his personality. Besides, look at his record.

B: Well, that's not so hot. We've still got bombs, we still hang people, the roads are full of drunks and imports from South Africa are higher than ever.

A: And what's more, we are against Bishops and he's a priest.

GIRL: Ah yes, but he objected strongly to the election of Dr Robert Stopford as Bishop of London. He said the procedure was a relic of a bygone age and he faced jail, outlawry and the confiscation of all his goods and chattels.

A: But he never went to jail, he isn't outlawed and he's got all his goods and chattels and who's Bishop of London? Dr Robert Stopford.

GIRL: Yes, but the main thing is that he did protest. He spoke up. He stood up for what he believed, never mind the consequences. He took on authority single-handed. And he made the headlines.

B: All the same, it might be an embarrassment to have a priest in the organisation. After all, we aim to attract teenagers.

GIRL: But that's no problem. He said the church fusses too much about fornication.

A: But is he sufficiently with it?

GIRL: Of course he is. He put on a jazz show at the Royal Festival Hall to raise funds for Christian Action.

B: But nobody went. The prices were too high. He had to apologise. Said the organisation was muddled and that he knew nothing about jazz. Always in a muddle.

GIRL: But he enjoys it all so much. It's all such fun. I mean—that iron grey hair, those spectacles steaming with emotion, those fine, strong legs marching as to war. (*She suddenly collects herself.*) I'm sure that the very young find him very—er, er—fascinating.

B: Perhaps that's why he tried to ban the Lolita film before it was even made. We don't want to be associated with that kind of protest.

GIRL: But at least it showed that he had read the book.

A: His roots are too deep in the Establishment for my liking. He says he was a Tory until he was 31, which is a bit late in the day to see the light. And wasn't he (*he hisses*) a priest-in-ordinary to the King?

GIRL: But that was way back in 1934. He showed where his loyalties lay at the time of the Coronation. And in a way which fits in with our drunken drivers campaign.

A: What did he say?

GIRL: He said: 'How can we honestly take part in the Coronation ceremonies and remain satisfied to let so many people, including young children, be slaughtered on the roads?'

A and B: Oh!

B: But he was an RAF chaplain during the war. Did he bless the bombers?

GIRL: He may have done. But he was against compulsory parades.

B: Do you think he's vigorous enough? I mean—well—all those apologies he's had to make. And that charge of obstruction. The Bow Street magistrate dismissed it. Why?

A: Well, he said he didn't call the copper who arrested him a bloody fool.

B: That's what I mean. Why didn't he?

A: Would we be able to work with him? Pat Arrowsmith and Michael Scott resigned from the Council of the CND because they lost confidence in him as chairman.

GIRL: Oh they're just trouble-makers.

B: But Bertrand Russell said he found it impossible to work with him.

GIRL: Look, I don't think we should bring his name into an argument. Besides, he often speaks in parables.

A *and* B *murmur agreement.*

B: But you still can't explain away those apologies. He even had to apologise to the Southern Rhodesian government for mis-statements in an advertisement attacking them. A lot of other people had to apologise because he'd used their names as well.

A: Surely the same thing happened when he appealed for funds after Sharpeville.

GIRL: The fact is he's so good at organisation that people let him sign their names to appeals. They trust him. He doesn't have to consult them on mere points or detail. They don't mind apologising now and then.

A: You've got a very good point there, Vanessa. It might make it easier.

B: I don't see what you mean.

A: Well, we could put his name down as a committee member without even bothering him.

GIRL: We could even make him chairman. We don't actually need to tell him. We'll just put his name down on the letter-head.

A: All in favour.

(*Carried unanimously.*)

## *FIRE*    John Antrobus

Night, a blazing tenement, a call for help. In a telephone kiosk a man on the phone. A gentleman hurries up to the box and wrenches the door open.

GENT: Are you phoning the fire-brigade?

*The cockney puts his hand over the mouthpiece and surveys his intruder disdainfully.*

COCKNEY: I don't think it's any of your business who I'm phoning . . .

GENT: Look here, there's a big fire. I've got to phone the fire-brigade at once.

*The gent goes to enter the box. The cockney stands in his way.*

COCKNEY: I haven't finished, have I?

GENT: It's not important whether you've finished . . . just give me the phone!

*Gent tries to grab the phone. Cockney holds it away.*

COCKNEY: I'm not getting through to you, am I?

GENT: Give me that phone . . . don't you realise . . . there are children trapped in that burning house. . . .

COCKNEY: Whose are they? Yours?

GENT: What does it matter whose children they are . . . never mind that now . . . look please. . . .

COCKNEY: That's better—please.

GENT: Please give me that phone at once!

COCKNEY: Why?

GENT: Why? Why? Because in that blazing house there are children . . . who I admit are not my children . . . never mind . . . they are children and they are trapped in a blazing fire.

COCKNEY: And you are worried about them?

GENT: Yes . . . yes I am deeply concerned about them. . . .

COCKNEY: How long you been worrying about them kids? Them kids up there in that blazing tenement up there?

GENT: Damn it all, man, don't be inhuman . . . I was passing . . . I saw the children trapped in the fire. . . .

COCKNEY: They been up there a long while longer than that . . . them kids . . . them family's in that old tenement . . . they been in there for years . . . oh . . . it's a bit late

to start caring now, int it? Just suddenly start caring . . . you didn't care before the fire started did you?

GENT: I didn't know them before the fire started.

COCKNEY: You don't know 'em now . . . that's what I'm saying, int it?

GENT: Yes . . . yes of course I agree . . . I agree we must launch a massive slum clearance campaign . . . as soon as possible I've always said that . . . look please give me that phone. . . .

COCKNEY: By 'as soon as possible' I take it you mean as soon as the country's resources make it possible?

GENT: That's it yes. . . .

COCKNEY: You weren't making yourself quite clear on that point. . . .

*The gent makes another lunge for the phone. The cockney pushes him back.*

COCKNEY: Got any rats in your house have you?

GENT: No, I haven't. . . .

COCKNEY: No that couldn't wait could it . . . if you had a rat in your house it couldn't wait for 'as soon as possible' . . . that couldn't wait till the country's resources make it possible . . . anything your lot want don't wait for 'as soon as possible' . . . you have it when you want it, no messing. But us, mate . . . we're always waiting for as soon as possible . . . up in that tenement, mate, that's been condemned for fifty years . . . they been waiting to be re-housed 'as soon as possible' for fifty years up there.

GENT: Oh my God. . . .

COCKNEY: 'Ere tell you what. . . . Perhaps them kids'll use the fire escape eh . . . they might get one of them Duke of Edinburgh's awards eh . . . for initiative . . . you believe in initiative don't you? You back the Duke on that?

GENT: It so happens I do . . . but the point is . . .

COCKNEY: I thought you'd back the Duke on that ... I didn't think you'd go against the Duke on that ... that's what I mean, see....

*Gent suddenly loses all control and leaps at cockney, lashing out with his umbrella.*

GENT: Damn you! Damn you for a bolshevik! Get out of my way!

COCKNEY: I'm fed up getting out the way of people like you....

GENT: Get out of my way!

*Cockney shoves the gent off, and gent collapses onto the ground. We hear approach of fire-engines. The exhausted gent becomes aware of this, and pulls himself up on to his knees.*

GENT: The fire-engines ... they're here ... yes, thank God, they're in time.... (*Turns to cockney*) Somebody else called them ... you ... you filthy swine....

COCKNEY: Yeah. Yeah, it was me.

*He pushes the telephone receiver into the gent's hands and walks off*

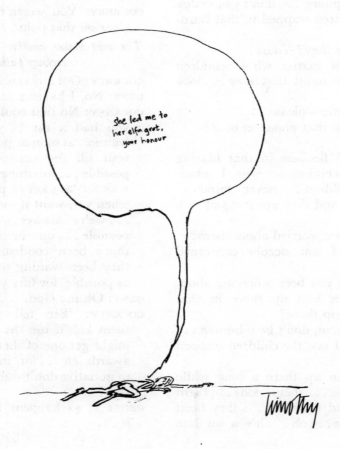

she led me to her elfin grot, your honour

Timothy

## THIS IS YOUR LIFE, HENRY BROOKE

David Frost & Christopher Booker

VERBATIM REPORT OF a special edition of this esteemed programme, broadcast on 30th March, 1963.

*This is Your Life, Henry Brooke. You were born Home Secretary a few short months ago . . . on Friday, 13th July 1962. Of all the many tributes that have been paid to you for your work on behalf of your fellow-man, perhaps the best-known and most sincere came from Mr Marcus Lipton, Labour MP for Brixton:*

LIPTON: "You are the most hated man in Britain."

*Henry—you had only been born Home Secretary for six days when . . . do you remember this voice. . . .*

CARMEN BRYAN: Henry wanted me to be the first to be emigrated under the new Immigration Act.

*Yes, Henry, that was the voice of Carmen Bryan, whom you haven't seen in the flesh—ever.*

CARMEN: The first time I heard of Henry was when I was put in prison for six weeks. I'd stolen goods worth £2 but it was my first offence and Henry thought that it was very serious. So he said he was going to deport me.

*Can you remember what you said to the House of Commons, Henry?*

HENRY: "I think it would be a great act of injustice if I were to stand in the way of her returning to Jamaica."

*Did you really? Anything else?*

HENRY: "I am not prepared to look at this case again."

*And for four days, Henry, you stood firm. And then on July 23rd, do you remember what you said?*

HENRY: "I am certain it would be wrong to impose on a person convicted of shoplifting both the experience of six weeks in prison and the penalty of deportation against her will."

*Your word, Henry, isn't very eloquent, is it? Hardly worth keeping at all. But you were going to deport her?*

HENRY: Yes, we were going to send her back where she came from.

*And where was that?*

HENRY: Brixton.

*But you did it all, Henry, to protect the nation's interests.*

HENRY: Oh, yes—my country—white and wrong.

*And then, on July 29th this voice was heard in a field in Gloucestershire:*

VOICE: Sieg Heil.

*Yes, the voice of George Lincoln Rockwell, the American Nazi Leader, recorded in Britain on July 29th. Two days later you announced that George Lincoln Rockwell would be officially banned from entering Britain. But August 1962, was a busy time for you, Henry. Do you remember this voice?*

VOICE: Save me, save me.

*Yes, you have a broad back, Henry, and you turned it on Robert Soblen. Unfortunately Dr Soblen cannot be with us tonight—but you remember, Henry—he was a convicted spy and a dying man. The Americans demanded his return, and he fled here from Israel and asked for the traditional right of political asylum. But to you, Henry, there were more important things than tradition. . . .*

HENRY: Yes, I am sure that when the full facts are revealed, you will agree that I was acting in the best interests of this country. By acting in the best interests of the United States of America.

*You decided not only that he couldn't stay but even where he'd got to go. You told the House of Commons. . . .*

HENRY: "Directions have been given to the airline for Dr Soblen's removal to the United States. He is fit to travel and I must act as I have said I will."

*Alas, Henry, Dr Soblen took an overdose of drugs—and let you down. Now, do you remember this voice?*

VOICE: Defense de gate-cracher.

*Yes, it's the voice of George Bidault. What was it you said about him to the House of Commons, do you remember?*

HENRY: "I have no grounds for thinking that Mr Bidault is now in this country."

ENTER BIDAULT

*Well, Henry, it's happened again. And what was it you said last time M. Bidault was here?*

HENRY: "My permission for him to enter the country was neither sought nor granted."

BIDAULT: Understandable, huh?

*And so, Henry, to this week and the case of Chief Enaharo, the Nigerian Opposition Leader who has asked for asylum but whom you are sending back into danger. He got in without you noticing him— like Rockwell and Bidault. You've changed your mind—as you did with Carmen Bryan. And you've ignored the spirit of British tradition to please another government—like Soblen. Your policy, Mr Brooke, has been one of trial and error. Their trials. Your errors. On behalf of us all—particularly of Dr Soblen and Chief Enaharo—THIS IS YOUR LIFE, HENRY BROOKE—and was theirs.*

HENRY: Just shows. If you're Home Secretary—you can get away with murder.

## THIS'LL KILL YOU    Peter Lewis & Peter Dobereiner

FOR 43 YEARS now I've been selling carcinogens. Not wittingly, mind you. Not wittingly for all that time. When I first took this kiosk there wasn't any harm in tobacco. People smoked . . . and died . . . and nobody kept on at them about it. So I didn't worry unduly when the first scare started just after the war. There's always somebody trying to spoil other people's pleasures.

Then the General Medical Council looked into it and said there wasn't any doubt about it whatever. *And* the Government accepted their report. Well . . . I was worried for a time. Not for myself, mind, I don't smoke, but I felt sorry for all those rats and mice. Besides, this kiosk is my living. But as it turned out, I needn't have worried at all. My takings actually went up that year.

One of my customers would have his little joke. 'Death sentences,' he'd say. 'That's what you're selling. There ought to be a law against people like you,' he said when he came to collect his box of fifty every morning. Very comical character. I was sorry to see him go. I said to Doris after the funeral, I said, 'Supposing they did pass a law? What ought we to do?'

'Don't you worry,' she said. 'Just you wait till the Government tells us what to do. Course they'll stop you selling fags if they're harmful,' she said, 'but they'll give us compensation. You can trust the Government.' That was her favourite phrase, God rest her soul. She put her head in the gas oven when her bit of War Loan fell to 53.

A year or two went by and no-one made any announcement so I took the problem to our MP. A more straightforward man you could not hope to meet. 'Don't you worry, Armitage,' he said. 'The Government won't ban the sale of tobacco for one very good reason,' he said. 'Because it would be interfering with the liberty of the subject. There's twenty million smokers in the country,' he said. 'Now would it be fair to *them*? There is also the consideration that the tobacco tax brings in £800 million a year which is fourteen per cent of the annual revenue and we just couldn't carry on without it.'

When he put it like that, I could see it was my patriotic duty to keep the kiosk open. If we closed down you wouldn't have no hydrogen bombs and that. If you look at it, as these MPs do, impartially, 26,000 deaths a year from lung cancer is a small price to pay for the liberty of the subject *plus* a nuclear stockpile.

Twenty-six thousand people represents the population of quite a small town, like Newbury, say. Ah! I can see what you're thinking: Newbury last year, Windsor this year, Abingdon, Wallingford, Lambourn, Streatley and Pangbourne next year . . . a few more years and we'll have got through the whole of Berkshire. But it's no use running away from the facts. Berkshire, pleasant as it is, has to be weighed against the long-term welfare of the country as a whole.

So I don't worry, and if you take my tip you won't worry either.

You've got the law on your side. You've got the Government behind you. And you're making your contribution to the defence of Britain and the cause of liberty for which so many of your fellow-smokers have not hesitated to lay down their lives.

## AN ORDINARY FAMILY AT HOME    Brian Glanville

*Come with us to Hatfield to meet an ordinary family—the McCorquodales and the Dartmouths; or, as they are better known, the Barbara Cartlands and the Mrs Gerald Legges. Ordinary women with ordinary interests; clothes, homes, children, prisons, dirty cups and saucers, husbands, sewers, vitamin pills. And with views on all these things, views which frequently find their way into the newspapers. Every quote guaranteed.*

MRS LEGGE: The Westminster sewers are vastly superior to those old LCC ones.

Q: But what does Lord Dartmouth think?

MRS LEGGE: My husband's idea of misery would be to be told details of the Westminster sewers.

Q: The great thing about Lady Dartmouth and her mother is that they got on together as *ordinary* mothers and daughters do.

MRS LEGGE: Mummy and I have no secrets at all.

Q: And how would Mrs McCorquodale describe her daughter?

BARBARA CARTLAND: Beautiful, vivacious, hard working and adorable.

Q: Ordinary people, with ordinary views.

BARBARA CARTLAND: I think there is too much fuss made about the pains of childbirth; it isn't as bad as all that.

MRS LEGGE: Nothing is more degrading, more humiliating, more completely contrary to one's whole conception of a man than to see him in a plastic apron.

Q: What does Lord Dartmouth think?

MRS LEGGE: His views are absolutely clear. I can rely on them.

BARBARA CARTLAND: Love-making should begin over the dinner table, with soft words and a kiss. It shouldn't just start at bedtime.

Q: What does Lord Dartmouth think?

MRS LEGGE: Men haven't changed at all. They're all cavemen at heart.

BARBARA CARTLAND: Public schoolboys, of course, learn old-fashioned courtesy. So naturally they get better jobs.

MRS LEGGE: Often I found that where Socialist voters lived, there were dirty milk bottles on the doorstep.

Q: Lady Dartmouth has seen something of life in the raw.

MRS LEGGE: Once, when I was doing missionary work at Vauxhall Bridge, I spoke to a man who was an alcoholic.

Q: How does Lord Dartmouth feel?

MRS LEGGE: He's the most heavenly person.

Q: As a romantic novelist, what does Miss Cartland feel is the basis of a happy marriage?

BARBARA CARTLAND: It is a wise wife who remembers that if she wants a young, vigorous, exciting husband, she must see that he gets meat and two veg each day.

MRS LEGGE: No love is ever wasted.

BARBARA CARTLAND: Once you couldn't walk down a street alone without being pounced on. Now you could walk out in the nude, and no man would give you a glance.

MRS LEGGE: I think British men are wonderful—so much more attractive than Continentals.

BARBARA CARTLAND: But of course the American man is a better housewife.

116

Q: What other advice would Miss Cartland give to wives?

BARBARA CARTLAND: Wash yourself in honey. It's awfully healthy.

MRS LEGGE: I always use boot polish. Boot polish is responsible for making our eyelashes so long and silky.

Q: Ordinary people, with ordinary concerns; the sort of things that concern you and me.

BARBARA CARTLAND: The Post Office, for instance, are as rude as they can possibly be to anybody. If they talk as they do to people like me—you know, top people, proprietors —goodness knows what they say to old age pensioners.

Q: People with ordinary feelings.

MRS LEGGE: Actually it always upsets me dreadfully to find someone doesn't like me. It always seems to me to be so unfair of them. I always, always make an effort to be pleasant and I have never given anyone any cause to dislike me.

Q: Of course, Lord Dartmouth would agree. Lord Dartmouth . . .? Lord Dartmouth . . .! Oh, never mind.

## CONRAD HILTON     Peter Lewis & Peter Dobereiner

IN THE BEGINNING there was darkness upon the face of the earth and there was no iced water. And Hilton said, Let there be iced water, and in every bathroom pipes ran with plenteous iced water and Hilton saw that it was good. Then he said, Let there be music, and in every lobby, single studio parlour, double French bedroom and luxury suite, nay, in every elevator, other pipes gushed with plenteous canned music. And Hilton said, Let the earth bring forth Hiltons, yielding fruit after their kind. And the El Paso Hilton begat the Beverly Hilton, which begat the Puerto Rico Hilton which begat the Istanbul Hilton which begat the Panama Hilton which begat the Berlin Hilton which begat the Nile Hilton which begat the Virgin Isle Hilton which begat the Trinidad Hilton which begat the Teheran Hilton which begat the Acapulco Hilton and on the seventh day Hilton rested . . . but only for a moment.

For messengers came unto him and said, Behold, there is an Anglo-Saxon people that dwell in darkness and know not thy name, nor drink they of thine iced water. And Hilton took his rod and smote upon the rock in the place which is called Park Lane and out of it came forth a pillar of 130,000 cubic feet of concrete. And the view from the top thereof was thirty miles in any direction and from thirty miles in any direction thereof the view was, alas, of the pillar.

Then sent Hilton for the scribes and elders of the people and commanded them to come to him. And they cast lots and sent unto him an elder named Maudling whom they could best spare to be sacrificed. And he gave him a pair of silver scissors and bade him cut the tape, and Maudling would not. But the serpent Clore, who privily did own the freehold, tempted his handmaiden, Beryl, and she spake unto Maudling saying, Give me the scissors. And lo, as he stood pondering as was his wont, what words to speak, she cut the tape and there was a great gushing of iced water and puking of piped music and a great charging of fifty guineas a night without breakfast.

And Hilton said, Behold I have given unto you the London Hilton containing everything meet for your needs: a view into the garden of your Queen, yea, and a library wherein ye may read Hilton Milton and 850 Hilton menservants and maidservants smiling Hilton smiles, which they smile not saying cheese, as other men, but saying Hilton Stilton.

But the people were a stiff-necked people who would not drink of the iced water nor would they eat of the Olde English Breakfast, consisting of ripe melon, All Bran, Crisp waffles with ham or sausage and hot chocolate. For they cried out, What is this Olde English Breakfast, for we know it not, neither will we pay 15s. 6d. for it.

And Hilton was exceeding wrath and departed with a gnashing of teeth to beget the Athens Hilton which begat the Moscow Hilton which was called the Comrade Hilton which begat the Pisa Hilton, which was called the Tiltin' Hilton which begat the Tel Aviv Hilton which was called the Hilton Schmilton, which begat the Rabat Hilton and doubtless also the Sodom Hilton and the Gomorrah Hilton which were also turned into pillars of concrete. And it came to pass that the Hiltons covered the face of the earth and there was a great flood of iced water and the darkness was greater than it was in the beginning.

# 8 Two People in Four Situations

## I

*Everyone's Depressing Basically*

HE: Come on, then.

SHE: What?

HE: We're going to visit Ethel and Victor.

SHE: Oh no, really, I couldn't face it.

HE: Why not?

SHE: They're so badly adjusted. Really, we'll just be all upset.

HE: But we promised.

SHE: Well, I'm not up to it.

HE: But Clive and Sally'll be there.

SHE: Oh, no. She'll never let him tell a joke, and he'll look like a little lost lamb.

HE: But David'll be there.

SHE: Don't say any more, I'll cry. Why are all our friends so depressing? Honestly, I couldn't face it.

HE: Well, we can stay home then.

SHE: Uh-huh.

HE: I'll put the telly on.

SHE: No.

HE: Why not?

SHE: It's too depressing.

HE: It's 'Panorama'.

SHE: I know. I don't think I could stand that.

HE: What are you talking about?

SHE: I don't want the television on. I don't want all those unhappy people in my house.

HE: What unhappy people? Richard Dimbleby, for heaven's sake.

SHE: Richard Dimbleby for one. I've got my own troubles, thank you.

HE: There's nothing wrong with Richard Dimbleby.

SHE: No, oh?

HE: No.

SHE: I suppose you haven't noticed his figure.

HE: His figure?

SHE: He's fat. He eats too much. Compensation. He's a very unhappy man, Jimmy.

HE: Come on.

SHE: I'd just rather not watch.

HE: Well, all right. I just thought . . .

SHE: All these sick people with their petty problems. I just can't cope with it any more.

HE: Well, what about 'Monitor'? You used to watch that?

SHE: Huw Wheldon. (*As if she had said 'Syphilis'.*)

HE: What's wrong with Huw Wheldon?

SHE: He's basically sour, that's all. There's something fundamentally wrong with him, that's all.

HE: Janet!

SHE: A nasty, envious man. It's all in the eyes, those darting looks, don't think I can't see it all.

HE: For heaven's sake! What about 'Sunday Night at the London Palladium'? Norman Vaughan.

SHE: A thin, nervous neurotic.

HE: We could watch an Animal Programme.

SHE: Grahame Dangerfield. (*More distasteful than 'Syphilis'.*)

HE: Well, what's wrong with Grahame Dangerfield?

SHE: Nothing, if you admire a man who is totally incapable of maintaining a human relationship.

HE: Nonsense.

SHE: Well, have you ever seen him with another human being in your life? No. Always turtles, budgies, otters.

HE: Well . . .

SHE: I never trust beards anyhow. They're always covering up insecurities.

HE: All right, all right. We could watch 'Come Dancing'.

SHE: Poor wasted souls. People who never read a book in their lives.

HE: All right, you win. Let's go to the pictures. (*Gets newspaper*)

SHE: What's on?

HE: There's 'Cat on a Hot Tin Roof' at the Classic. Elizabeth Taylor.

SHE: Home-wrecker. I wouldn't go to see that woman if . . .

HE: 'The Old Man and the Sea'. Spencer Tracy?

SHE: Have you noticed the lines on that man's face?

HE: 'The Password is Courage'.

SHE: Dirk Bogarde?

HE: Uh huh.

SHE: That weak, guilty mouth. What's he hiding anyhow?

HE: Danny Kaye as Hans Christian Andersen.

SHE: When is he going to grow up?

HE: (*Throwing down paper.*) All right! We could listen to the radio. There's Edmundo Ros. . . .

SHE: That pitiful refugee. It's all so unbearably depressing.

HE: Now stop that. This is ridiculous. (*Looks at watch.*) Holy cow, I didn't realise how late it was. We won't catch anything but the Epilogue. Can I put it on?

SHE: If you must.

HE: (*Switches on. Music from set, both watch.*) Oh look. It's the Reverend John Hamilton Duxtable.

SHE: (*Sadly looking at screen.*) If only there were some way we could help him!

II

*Nobel Prizes*

The announcement of the lucky winners on the Alfred Nobel Peace Pools is not an entirely happy occasion. For everyone who wins there are hundreds who lose.

R.: I see where the Nobel Prizes are gone.

M.: Oh yeh.

R.: Nabbed, every last one of 'em.

M.: Uh-huh.

R.: Four British scientists got 'em.

M.: Mmmmm.

R.: Max Perutz got one.

M.: Oh, did he? Max Perutz, eh?

R.: Yes, for haemoglobin.

M.: Oh.

R.: John Kendrew's got one.

M.: Is that so?

R.: Protein Myoglobin. Composition of the atoms.

M.: Fascinating.

R.: Francis Crick and Maurice Wilkins both got 'em.

M.: Uh-huh.

R.: Study of chromosomes transmitting messages to living tissues.

M.: You don't say.

R.: All gone. All the Nobel Prizes. There's an American got one. (*Silence.*) I say there's an American got one.

M.: Oh yes?

R.: J. D. Watson.

M.: Oh really? Little J. D. Watson. Who'd have thought he'd ever get the Nobel Prize? Makes you think, doesn't it.

R.: All gone. Every flippin' Nobel Prize.

M.: Uh-huh.

R.: And I didn't get one. Not one. Not even a mention.

M.: Just like last year.

R.: That's right.

M: Well, it's not surprising, is it?

R.: Not surprising?

M.: Well, you're not a scientist, are you?

R.: That's right. Rub salt in the wounds. You don't know that this means to me: Just look at this year, what a record I've got. I didn't win a gold medal at Perth.

M.: Or a silver.

R.: Or a bronze.

M.: You weren't there, were you?

R.: I was counting on that Nobel Prize. I thought that this year for sure. I had the feeling they were going to pick me. Why didn't they pick me? What made them change their minds?

M.: Maybe they forgot.

R.: They forgot last year. They can't just keep forgetting. There's something suspicious going on. I think they're avoiding me.

M.: That must be it.

R.: It wouldn't be so bad if no one in England had got it. But four British scientists, four!

M.: Mmmm.

R.: I came so close!

M.: You're gonna be late for work. (*Rising to get his jacket and lunchbox.*)

R.: Work! All those people! All knowing I didn't get the prize.

M.: That's life.

R.: (*Getting into jacket as she holds it.*) The jeers, the jibes . . .

M.: Don't take it too hard.

R.: And it's a whole year before I get another chance.

M.: (*Giving him box.*) Don't forget your lunch. Bye. (*They kiss.*) And cheer up. (*As he goes.*) There's always the Academy Award.

### III

### *Naked Films*

SHE: You've been again.

HE: I haven't.

SHE: You have. You've been again.

HE: I don't know what you're talking about.

SHE: Oh no, of course you don't.

HE: I haven't been.

SHE: I don't know why you do it. Sneaking in here with guilt written all over your face.

HE: Nonsense.

SHE: Deny it if you can. You've been to naked films all afternoon.

HE: What if I have?

SHE: (*Consulting small notebook.*) Two-fifty-eight, entered Gala Royal to see 'Naked as Nature Intended'. Three-thirty, down to the Cameo Moulin for 'My Bare Lady'. Four-fifteen, out of the Cameo Moulin and a number 13 bus across town to catch 'Some Like it Naked'.

HE: Nude.

SHE: What?

HE: 'Some Like it Nude'.

SHE: Oh. (*Makes correction in her book.*) Right. Then back across town by taxi this time, (*conversationally*) that must have cost a pretty penny. My fare came to seven bob, (*back to notebook*) and once more into 'Naked as Nature Intended'. Out of 'Naked as Nature Intended', across into a Wimpy for a Whippsy, and back to 'My Bare Lady' at five-o-seven. Out again at five-o-nine.

HE: The newsreel was on.

SHE: And over to 'Sun Lover's Paradise' at the Berkeley. Out at five-thirty and over to a Wimpy for a Whippsy and a Wimpy and back to 'Naked as Nature Intended'.

HE: Well you've spent a busy afternoon.

SHE: Aren't you ashamed of yourself? In and out of nude pictures all day.

HE: Me? What about you, then, flipping around after me in bleedin' taxis? Waitin' on the street corners eyein' the doors for my appearance. Following me at tremendous expense, I believe I heard the sum of . . .

SHE: Seven shillings.

HE: For taxi alone. And Lord only knows what else in bribes to loose-tongued Wimpy waitresses anxious to reveal their sordid secrets.

SHE: Oh, come on.

HE: I had a sausage, too.

SHE: When?

HE: In the cinema. At the Cameo Moulin, second trip.

SHE: How often have you seen 'Naked as Nature Intended'?

HE: I've lost count.

SHE: Is it good, then?

HE: How do you mean?

SHE: You know. Well acted.

HE: Oh it's reasonably well acted. For a nudist film. Performed more than acted, I'd say. I mean, your Ralph Richardsons aren't liable to show up in 'Naked as Nature Intended'. I mean your young Ralph Richardsons and Edith Evanses are not to be found in the nude films you understand.

SHE: No?

HE: Definitely not. I mean no budding Laurence Oliviers are liable to turn up in 'My Bare Lady'.

SHE: Well, is it well written?

HE: Not bad, not bad. Again it's not your vintage Rattigan, now is it? But then that's not what you're goin' for, is it? It's quite pleasant in its own way, quite distinctive, but not gripping, if you follow me. (*Laughs.*) If you follow me. (*She doesn't get it. He tries to explain through his laughter that the joke is that she followed him all afternoon. She doesn't get it. He gives up.*)

SHE: Well what's the big attraction then?

HE: Well, if pressed, I'd say the photography. Yes, the photography's definitely the main attraction.

SHE: Is it well photographed, then?

HE: No, no, it's pretty rotten actually.

SHE: Well how is it that you've been to see 'Naked as Nature Intended' in whole or in part, for a minimum of three and maximum of seven times each Sunday for the past eighteen weeks. November sixteen, five-seventeen, out at five-forty . . .

HE: All right. Do you mean you've been following me for the past four months?

SHE: Every Sunday. During which I may add you have consumed a total of thirty-two Wimpyburgers with and without cheese, and unknown Whippsys of various flavours.

HE: And you've got it all down in your little book?

SHE: Black on white.

HE: Every Sunday for eighteen weeks?

SHE: That's right.

HE: Well you have made me ashamed. I feel small and little. The thought of you waiting on all those corners Sunday after Sunday, for me to go in.

SHE: And come out!

HE: And come out. Tallying up the Wimpys.

SHE: As I fought against my own appetite.

HE: Dashing from end to end of town, from one naked cinema to another.

SHE: The ticket ladies know my face.

HE: Every week another. . . .

SHE: 'Nudes Round the World'.

HE: 'Mamzelle Striptease'.

SHE: 'The Fruit is Ripe'.

HE: 'Nudes in the Snow'.

SHE: 'Potemkin'.

HE: What?

SHE: An expensive mistake.

HE: Well, I'm cured. From now on I'm not wasting my life any longer. I've seen my last nude film.

SHE: You mean it?

HE: Absolutely. Never again will I step inside a naked cinema. The occasional Wimpy yes, but no more nudes.

SHE: You're sure?

HE: Yes.

SHE: (*Deflated.*) Oh. (*She tears up notebook.*)

HE: What's the matter?

SHE: I was just wondering what I'd do on Sundays from now on.

## Flybuttons

*A café. She has just finished her cup of coffee. He finished his long ago.*

M: (*Last sip of capuccino*) Well, that's nice.

R: Yes.

M: I wish you wouldn't do that.

R: What?

M: Eat mustard that way.

R: It's ketchup.

M: Well it'll be mustard in a minute. Or the vinegar. Why don't you order something if you're hungry?

R: I'm not hungry. You've got foam on your lips.

M: I've got what?

R: Foam on your lips.

M: Go on.

R: From the coffee.

M: Oh. (*She takes out mirror and wipes foam from her lips as daintily as she can manage with her fingers. Then she notices something and says awkwardly*)
Jimmy, bend your head close.

R: What?

M: Bend your head close, I want to whisper something.

R: You don't have to whisper.

M: I don't want no one to hear.

R: Nobody's going to hear. Nobody listening.

M: Well I don't want to say it loud.

R: Don't be daft.

M: Well I don't want to.

R: Come on.

M: (*Giggling*) Well I don't want to.

R: Just say it out loud.

M: (*Loud*) Your fly is open.

R: (*Hushed*) It's not.

M: (*Hushed*) It is.

R: (*His eyes glued to hers*) How far?

M: What do you mean how far?

R: How far is it open?

M: It's open more than half-way. Zip it up.

R: It buttons.

M: Well, button it up.

R: Why did you tell me?

M: What?

R: Why did you tell me it was open?

M: Stop eating that ketchup and button it up.

R: I don't want to.

M: Jimmy, for heaven's sake.

R: Now I am very curious about your motivations for telling me my fly is open.

M: Well . . . .

R: It strikes me as an aggressive and hostile action.

M: Hostile?

R: Obviously. I'm very embarrassed now.

R: What?

M: Eat mustard that way.

R: It's ketchup.

M: Well it'll be mustard in a minute. Or the vinegar. Why don't you order something if you're hungry?

R: I'm not hungry. You've got foam on your lips.

M: I've got what?

R: Foam on your lips.

M: Go on.

R: From the coffee.

M: Oh. (*She takes out mirror and wipes foam from her lips as daintily as she can manage with her fingers. Then she notices something and says awkwardly*) Jimmy, bend your head close.

R: What?

M: Bend your head close, I want to whisper something.

R: You don't have to whisper.

M: I don't want no one to hear.

R: Nobody's going to hear. Nobody listening.

M: Well I don't want to say it loud.

R: Don't be daft.

M: Well I don't want to.

R: Come on.

M: (*Giggling*) Well I don't want to.

R: Just say it out loud.

M: (*Loud*) Your fly is open.

R: (*Hushed*) It's not.

M: (*Hushed*) It is.

R: (*His eyes glued to hers*) How far?

M: What do you mean how far?

R: How far is it open?

M: It's open more than half-way. Zip it up.

R: It buttons.

M: Well, button it up.

R: Why did you tell me?

M: What?

R: Why did you tell me it was open?

M: Stop eating that ketchup and button it up.

R: I don't want to.

M: Jimmy, for heaven's sake.

R: Now I am very curious about your motivations for telling me my fly is open.

M: Well . . . .

R: It strikes me as an aggressive and hostile action.

M: Hostile?

R: Obviously. I'm very embarrassed now.

M: Well, button it up.

R: That's what you want, isn't it? Don't eat the ketchup, button your fly. You want to stamp out any individuality I've got, don't you? I wouldn't button that fly if it were open all the way.

M: It is now.

R: Maybe I like it open. Has that ever occurred to you? No, that didn't occur to you, because you're so bleedin' bourgeois.

M: Well, if it's bourgeois to button your fly. . . .

R: It's symptomatic.

M: Well, I'm sorry.

R: It's typical of your whole way of life.

M: I said I was sorry.

R: No courage, no conviction. What do you believe in? Go on, tell me, what do you believe in?

M: Oh, I don't know.

R: There it is. The backbone of our civilisation. 'I don't know.' What about Berlin then?

M: What?

R: Africa, Algeria? What are you doing about it? Nothing. Bloody nothing. You know what your answer to the world situation is, don't you. Button your fly.

M: Oh, Jimmy.

R. Oh it's sickening, sickening. Everything's all right isn't it as long as we button our flippin' flies.

M: I'm sorry.

R: Who cares if the world blows up, as long as we button our flies. That's it, isn't it, that's what you think?

M: We're gonna be late for the films.

R: That's what you think, isn't it, that's how your little mind works.

M: (*Getting up*) We're going to be late.

R: All right, all right. Just wait till I button my fly.

Steven Vinaver

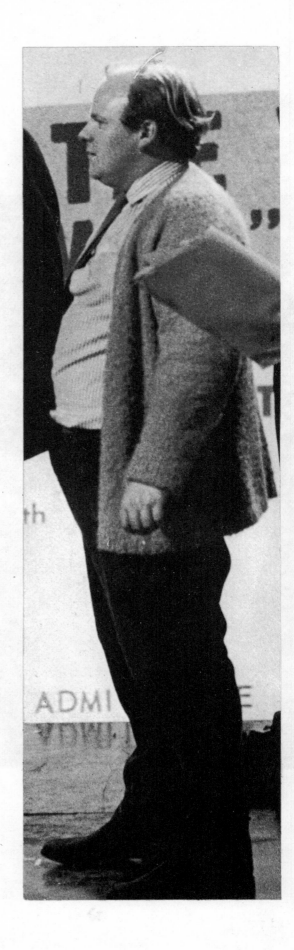

# 9 More Songs

**THREE SONGS**    Herbert Kretzmer

*Teenager*

The usual acknowledgements to Mr Noel Coward.

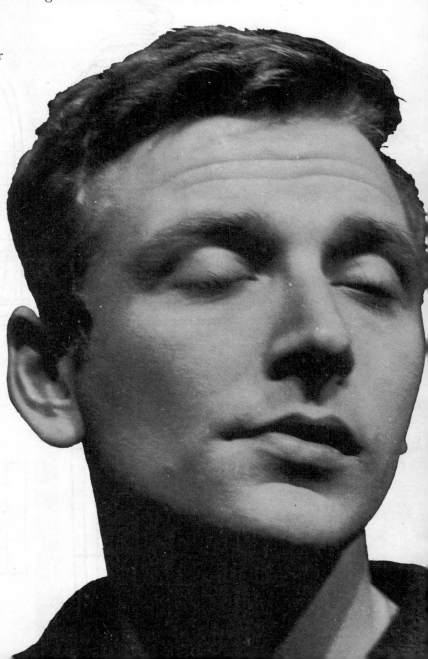

Teenager, teenager,
Living so *terribly* fast.
Selling your soul to the nearest bidder
Why don't you hesitate to consider
Where it may lead at last?

Glittering child of tender years,
Who's only half alive.
You've lost your precious honour
In clouds of marijuana.
In Greek Street
The urgent beat
Of saxophones throb 'til five.
No wonder half you beggars
Are preggers.

To tell the truth,
When I was a youth,
Temptations were much fewer.
We drank May wine
But toed the line
And kept ourselves quite pure.
For life devours
Our precious hours
And we've *terribly* few to spare!
Teenager, better beware!

Teenager, teenager,
Your life's a merry hell.
Come fill the flowing cup
And drink it.
You see yourself as just a
Trinket
And sin, a mere bagatelle!

Frivolous girl in frightful jeans,
Collecting scores of boys,
You'll add to your collection
All manner of infection.
In Soho
They sink so low
In their sad, erotic joys,
That if they're feeling seedy,
It's V.D.

It's a terrible town
When the sun goes down
And the junkie jazzman sings,
And you can't dismiss
The nemesis
That's waiting in the wings.

Before you rot
Cease your mad gavotte,
Or your end must be despair!
Teenager, better take care,
Teenager, better beware!

## *Lullaby for an Illegitimate Child*

*Sung by a young unmarried mother, probably in a Bayswater bedsitting room which is shaped like any letter of the alphabet between, say, E and O*

It must have been last April that it happened
I was dating Fred, and Ted, and Sid, and Lou.
But before the summer ended
I was visibly distended.
I know why, and so do you.

*This piece of brazenry done with, mother sings
the rest of the soothing chant directly to her
encribbed babe*

Conceived you may have been in sordid
   passion;
But, baby, you've arrived, and you're in
   fashion!

Don't you weep, my little baby,
'Cause you haven't got a dad.
Go to sleep, my little baby,
Things aren't really quite so bad.
There's no reason any longer
Why you ought to feel so blue.
The world is full of bastards
Just like you.

Don't you cry, my little baby,
Though it seems a crying shame
That you'll die, my little baby,
Never knowing what's your name.
There's no telling where you'll stop;
Lots of nature's children
Reach the top.

For example, good King Arthur
Likewise gallant Sir Gawain;
Not to mention both the Borgias
Not to mention Charlemagne.
Then there's Willi-am the Conqueror
And T. E. Lawrence, too;
And Adolf Hitler's father
Was a bastard through and through!

Four hundred thousand kiddies just as innocent
   as you
Were left behind by soldiers at the end of World
   War Two.

And now one in every eight of London's baby
   population
Has a mother who's a mother like your mother.
So smile your Mona Lisa smile, my dear mis-
   calculation.
(Which reminds me, Leonardo was another).

Learn to laugh, my little baby;
It won't always be a slur.
For the graph, my little baby,
Shows there's more of you each year.
And by the time you've grown up
And there's hair upon your chest
Why then, you lot could outnumber all the rest.

Papa was no bridegroom and your Mama was
   no bride
Yet sleep in peace, my angel baby,
Time is on your side.

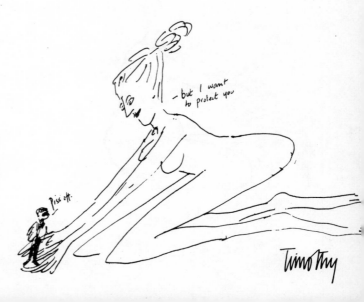

## Song of Nostalgia for an American State

*This song is sung by a lady in sequins, long black stockings and an Uncle Sam top hat, patriotically decorated. She is accompanied by Jolson-type minstrels. The whole enterprise is sung and performed with the energy and jollity proper to this kind of entertainment.*

LADY WITH THE TOP HAT SINGS (with much sentiment):

I wanna go back to Mississippi,
Where the scents of blossoms
Kiss the evenin' breeze,

Where the Mississippi mud
Kinda mingles with the blood
Of the niggers
Who are hangin'
From the branches of the trees.

I wanna go back to Mississippi
So, honey, don't be late—
Up above there's nuttin'
But a butter-coloured moon,
While down below
They're cuttin' up
A chocolate-coloured coon

So carry me back to Mississippi
That all-American state!

MINSTREL GROUP (with pride and fervour)

Mississippi is the state you gotta choose!
Where we hate all the darkies,
And the Cath'lics,
And the Jews—
Where we welcome any man
If he's white and strong
And belongs to the Ku-Klux-Klan!
Take me, take me
Home to Mississippi
That's the place I wanna be!
Miss you, Mississippi—
Mississippi, Land Of The Free!

ONE MINSTREL

Saw an uppity nigger
Goin' to cast his vote—
I took that uppity nigger
And cut his goddam throat

MINSTREL GROUP

Uppity, uppity nigger
Where you goin' today?
If you vote we'll cut your throat
Dooda, dooda day!

LADY WITH THE TOP HAT

I wanna go back to Mississippi
Where the scents of blossoms
Kiss the evenin' breeze

Where the Mississippi mud
Kinda mingles with the blood
Of the niggers
Who are hangin'
From the branches of the trees.

I wanna go back to Mississippi
Where everything's just great
And if you ain't for segregatin'
White folks from the black
Why, they won't
Hesitate to shoot you bravely in the back—
So carry me back to Mississippi
That All-American!
All-American!
All-American state!

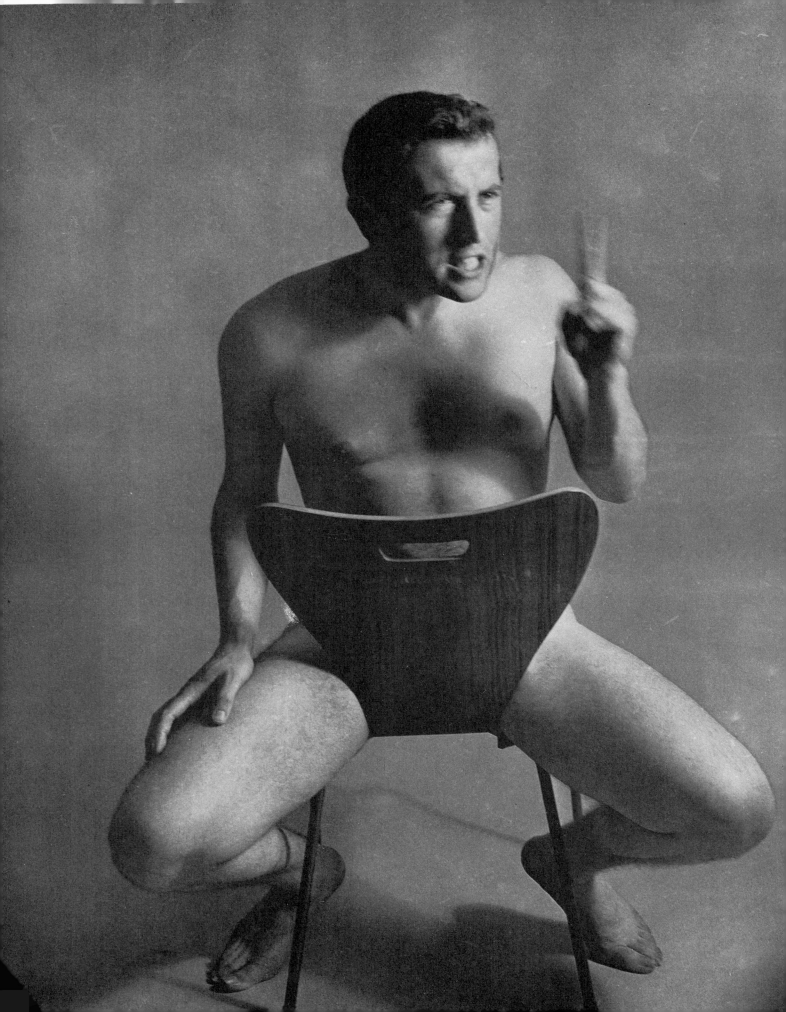

# 10 Press

## TEN COMMANDMENTS FOR JOURNALISTS

David Frost & Christopher Booker

DURING THE VASSALL TRIBUNAL the Government managed to transform an inquiry into their own bumbling incompetence into a witch-hunt against two unfortunate journalists and to lay down that the concealment of embarrassing facts was a criminal offence when committed by anyone but themselves. The Government's part was certainly inexcusable. But for Fleet Street, the whole affair was an excuse—an excuse to parade St Brendan and St Reginald as martyrs to the cause of the Divine Right and Writing of the Press.

It was followed by a special Service of Intercession for Journalists in St Bride's Church. Someone even suggested that they should have Ten Commandments all to themselves. Always eager to oblige . . .

1. Thou shalt have no other gods before fee.

2. Thou shalt not make unto thee any likeness of anything that is in the heaven above or that is in the earth beneath or that is in the water under the earth. Thou shalt invent the whole bloody lot.

3. Thou shalt not take the name of the Lord thy Boss in vain; for the Lord will hold him jobless that taketh his name in vain.

4. Remember the Sabbath Day to keep it holy; wholly unpleasant. Unless you're on the *Observer*, in which case, of course, remember the Sabbath Day to keep it woolly. For in six days the Lord made the *Daily Express* and the *Evening Standard*, and all that in them is. And on the Seventh Day he made the *Sunday Express*—wherefore the Lord blessed the Sabbath Day with John Gordon, the prophet Crossbencher and the dead loss Robert Pitman.

5. Honour thy father and mother of a hangover.

6. Thou shalt not kill stories, only reputations.

7. Thou shalt not omit adultery.

8. Thou shalt not steal stories unless they be from obscure foreign publications in which case thou shalt feel that thou wilt get away with it, in the eyes of the Lord and indeed of the Vassall Tribunal.

9. Thou shalt not bear false witness against thy neighbour; look what happened to *Private Eye*.

10. Thou shalt not covet thy neighbour's scoop—but thou shalt not be averse to lifting it out of the first editions. For thou knowest that soon thy Editor will be shouting not 'Where is Thy Original Manuscript?', but rather 'Where is Thy Copy?'

In short, there's no doubt that in Fleet Street's new mood of piety and principle the closing words of any service would undoubtedly be 'Publish—and Be Blessed'.

# THE SUNDAY TELEGRAPH     Peter Tinniswood

*THE SUNDAY TELEGRAPH is setting new fashions in journalism. Each Sunday it turns out its full battery of expert correspondents. They have an expert on every subject. . . .*

Freddie Trueman produced a superb 6 for 27 bowling performance, writes our cricket correspondent, at Hobart, Tasmania, writes our Commonwealth correspondent, on a perfect, sunny afternoon, writes our weather correspondent.

Yes, this was Fiery Fred at his most hostile, writes our military correspondent. On this delightful, pocket-sized ground set in a basin of gently-sloping green hills, writes our estates and property correspondent, Trueman got little help from a yellow and lifeless pitch, writes our agricultural correspondent.

His success stemmed from superbly-flighted pace bowling, writes our air correspondent, which had Tasmanian batsmen all at sea, writes our naval correspondent.

Undoubtedly, writes our political correspondent, England, writes our diplomatic correspondent, are learning, writes our education correspondent, that the fiery Yorkshireman, writes our Sheffield correspondent, is indispensable—which is more than can be said for E. W. Swanton, writes R. A. Roberts.

---

*In Vino Veritas !*

## JENNIFER   Peter Lewis & Peter Dobereiner

THE FIRST RULE young journalists learn on local papers is to get the names and spell them right. The great example to them all is a lady journalist who has inflated the practice of name-dropping to the proportions of a landslide—Jennifer, the society diarist of *The Queen*.

Here is a page of Jennifer's Diary. . . .      And here it is with the names left out

# JENNIFER'S DIARY          # JENNIFER'S DIARY

*Miss Juliet Ash and Mr. David Dixon who were married at All Saints, Narborough, Norfolk.*

*Pytchley Hunt Ball.*

*Pytchley Hunt Ball.*

Her versatility is a byword. Send her to any variety of social event and her style is equal to it. Here she is, for instance, at a wedding . . .

. . . Others present included the Countess of Portsmouth, Mrs R. B. B. B. Cooke and her daughter Mrs Ray Salter, Sir Frederick and Lady Hoare, Miss Mary Rose Hoare, Lt.-Col. and Mrs Hugh Brassey, Sir William and Lady Wrixon-Becher, Mrs Eileen Herbert and Lady Bonsor . . .

Whereas here, she attends a ball . . .

. . . Among others present were Lord Chesham, Sir Hendrie and Lady Oakshott (he won a large pink teddy bear on the tombola) Mr and Mrs Terence Morrison-Scott, Major and Mrs James Ford, the Hon. Mrs Burns, the Hon. Mrs Skyrme, Mr and Mrs Archie Black, Mr and . . .

And now, in dramatic contrast, she reports from a cattle show . . .

. . . Others present included Lord Elphinstone who goes in for this breed, Lt.-Col. Eion Merry and his very pretty wife, Mr John Arnott, Sir Kenneth and Lady Butt, Mr Thomas Fothringham . . .

How would you describe that style? *Consistent*, isn't it? I particularly like the striking variations of phraseology such as 'Among others present' and 'Others present included'.

*135*

And that by no means exhausts the possibilities. What about: '*Also present*' and even, on special occasions, '*Besides those I've already mentioned others present included*'. Those subtle changes of pace are not lost on Jennifer addicts.

She never gives any reason for being interested in these people, such as reporting anything they said or did. Why does she mention them? Because they were *there*. And also because it's faces and names that persuade advertisers to pay about twice as much for space in *The Queen* as the circulation justifies.

It's a punishing life, dropping names. One reader wrote in: 'I cannot wait to learn how many Jennifers there are. No one woman could keep up this pace'. To this she replied: 'Alas I have no exciting news for you of a team of Jennifers. I am alone. I often work a twenty-hour day several days a week. . . .' In fact, the reader might like to know, there isn't even one Jennifer. Her name is Betty, but they didn't call it Betty's diary presumably because it might have sounded so like the home life of our own dear Queen.

But what are these 20-hour days like? Hectic.

6.45 a.m. massage. Every morning I listen to the seven o'clock news, usually in my bath. From 8 a.m. onwards incoming calls (very delaying!) until I leave for the office where the telephone continues all day, mostly on the same lines: to fix a dance, where to have it, what band to have, how to contact a band, what caterers to use, where to get Queen Charlotte's Ball tickets, where to get Caledonian Ball tickets, how to get chosen for the Berkeley Dress Show, how many dresses does a girl need for the season, what theatres I'd advise for an old uncle up from Devon or a party of rather bright teenagers. . . . Where to buy old silver, how to set about chartering a yacht, how to announce an engagement, do I know a good temporary cook, how much does it cost to have a day's hunting with the Duke's or the Heythrop, how can you get a debutante's photograph published, have I heard of Mrs Baremile who has asked them to dine . . .

The morning, in short, is devoted to helping social climbers get their feet on the ladder. Once her clients are equipped with everything needed for civilised life, from Queen Charlotte's Ball tickets to a good temporary cook, there is nothing left to do but sit back and wait for their name to appear after those magic words 'Others present included'.

Jennifer has six regular Upper-class adjectives.

*Attractive*
For brides' mothers

*Charming*
For Bridegrooms' mothers

*Roomy*
For houses

*Useful*
For Horses

*Good*
For parties and . . .

*Splendid*
For charities and tombola prizes.

But suppose one day the hectic revelry gets out of hand and Jennifer finds herself on the spot in an emergency where, for once, she has to report something that is actually happening. How will she cope with a crisis?

... Tuesday. Hectic. Massage at 6.45. The telephone continued madly all day, mostly on the same lines: can Debrett be bribed, do I know the address of a good divorce lawyer, where to procure an abortion. On to Queen Charlotte's Ball, a really good dance and the last to be held in that roomy hotel, Grosvenor House, which has now been completely destroyed by fire. The party really warmed up when the able chairman, the late Lady Stevenage, lit the cake, as it had been filled with fireworks by the Hon. Boofy Fitzherbert and other young friends in the Guards, some of whom went on to spend the night at West End Central police station where I'm told one can get a really good massage. Several friends in the Red Cross and St John's Ambulance brought stretcher parties and others present included Divisional Superintendent Rudge, who arrived on that useful fire engine, the Leyland.

I saw that pretty debutante, the Hon. Penelope Vaughan, attractive in flame-coloured tulle, and her mother, radiant in tulle-coloured flame, make a very good jump from an upper window. They were unhappily not caught as the splendid tombola prizes were being drawn at that moment. Many other guests went on to St Thomas's Hospital whose ball is being held at the Park Lane Hotel on June 7.

Among other bleeding friends I saw Major and Mrs Villiers Bell, the Hon. Jeremy Ickeworth-Barton and Mr and Mrs Joseph Hammond-Gibbs.

The Earl and Countess of Stoke Newington who will not now be giving a dance for their late daughter on June 7th, please note. Others who perished included Nemone, Lady Withington, off to be laid out at Harrods, with Lt.-Col. and Mrs Charles Wimpole-Cavendish, Mr and Mrs Farquaharson-Pearse, The Laird of Clantilloch & Mrs Clantilloch, Mr and Mrs . . .

# The Bells Peal Out!

**BY DAVID FROST AND CHRISTOPHER BOOKER**

The best-kept secret of the year is out!

They're **ENGAGED** . . . Iris Greaves of Scunthorpe and Arthur Nast, also of Scunthorpe.

Even her best friends didn't know that this bubbling, fun-loving girl had finally settled on the man of her choice.

The cocoa was flowing in Gresham Road last night, the tops fizzing off the bottle of genuine champagne substitute. Iris—looking radiant and waving graciously, as Arthur got on the bus to go home.

**For years Iris's name has been linked with that of almost every unmarried man in Scunthorpe, except with the man of her choice, handsome Arthur Nast, who has had twenty-nine jobs in the past year.**

'This lovely, lively girl has won a special place in all our affections', said Mrs Mabel Turvey, aged eighty-two. **'She is marrying for love, as her mother always did.'**

The wedding will be held as soon as possible in the lovely centuries-old Scunthorpe registry-office.

Last night Arthur travelled to the Town Hall, to seek the consent of the Mayor, who replied, **'Push off, it's got nothing to do with me'.**

## *HULLO FANS*   John Wells & James Crossman

. . . Well here we are in the seventh round of this World Heavyweight Boxing Contest, between Lars Krupp of Denmark and Beaumont St John Ffoulkes, the plucky English lad from Leamington Spa, which is being slogged out here under the glare of television lights at the Empress Hall. There's a wonderful atmosphere of gaiety and excitement. The Danish boy has a very nasty cut over his right ear, which has been opening up very nicely during the last two rounds; both eyes have now closed up altogether, his jaw is broken in four places, and his nose has been hammered completely flat. Which means that those big right arm swingers from the English boy are really coming home to roost. But it's not all roses for the English boxer either; his skull was badly fractured when he was knocked out of the ring in the second round, he seems to have lost the use of his left arm, which means that his left ear is now showing signs of wear and tear: and Krupp's last piledriver to the solar plexus had him looking really stupid. I was going to say 'If only his mother could see him now', but I see that Mrs Ffoulkes is in fact in her usual seat at the ringside and she's not enjoying it one little bit. And I can't say I'm surprised: both boys have been down four times, Krupp for a count of eight and Ffoulkes for nine, but they are both gluttons for punishment. They've both got bags of guts and it's just a question whether one of them can pull something out of the bag for the last few minutes of this bitter bloody battle; and my word the fans are really getting their money's worth.

But it looks as though one of the contestants has thrown in the towel: the referee has come to a decision: I think he's holding up an arm . . . yes, he's holding up an arm!

WITH THE *Kama Sutra* and the *Naked Lunch* and Henry Miller entering the best sellers lists immediately after being reviewed in the posh Sundays and the weeklies, it can't be long before the entire spring list of those under-the-counter Parisian publishers reaches the bookshops over here. Followed, undoubtedly, by regular reviews in the highbrow papers of:

# The Week's Pornography

In a dull week the best of an indifferent bunch is *Lustful Loins* by Madam 'X' (surely a pseudonym?), an astringent, picaresque novella with overtones of Frank Harris and the undertones of the Marquis de Sade. Despite its obvious debt to Count 'Z's' *Joy of the Flesh* and possibly to J. D. Salinger, it is an original work standing head and shoulders above the very derivative *Lady Chatterley's Mother*, which my colleague Marghanita Laski reviewed last week. *Lustful Loins* is set in a Normandy castle and its environs. Its anti-heroine, Lady 'Y'—less scrupulous than Lewis Eliot, more female than Lucky Jim—moves through a loose, plotless series of incidents, each one vividly etched, involving members of the aristocracy, servants, dwarfs and farmyard stock. Despite some tiresome mannerism in style (such as the frequent use of the word 'throbbing') Madam 'X' is a born writer and I predict that her book will eventually take its place alongside the until recently under-rated *Memoirs of a Strict Governess*.

Pamela Fettish is a writer who seldom disappoints, but alas! her latest confection, *Silk Knickers*—a comedy of errors in which a young cabinet minister finds himself mistaken for a lady's maid—is tiresome and repetitive. It's all been done before, Miss Fettish! The incident with the fifteen-year-old butcher's boy, apparently based on fact, was described far more graphically and far more succinctly in Bow Street Magistrates' Court four years ago.

Another writer who appears to lean on fact is a new author called Nicholas Camp, the latest recruit from the thriving northern school of mucky books. His first novel, *The Young Gods*, describing his adventures among the cadaverous aesthetes of the Carlisle College of Further Education, has an eerie, fin-de-siècle quality about it; especially in the climax—a riotous description of a party at the house of one Gerald, in which the author (the book is written in the first person) finds himself chained in the cellar. But this is obviously an autobiographical work and it remains to be seen what Mr Camp can do when he has finished his sentence.

About *The Typist's Honeymoon* the least said the better. Anonymously written, badly produced—it appears to have been run off on an office Gestetner—it is nothing more than a hashed-up version of *The Secretary's Honeymoon*. And the proof-reading is appalling.

(*Next week Cyril Connolly will review the Little Magazines*—RITZY STORIES, GIRLIE and FRENCH KISS.)

# N O N Reader's Digest

All 1963

**THE WORLD'S SLOWEST CIRCULATION**
Over 23 Million Copies in 13 Languages Bought by Readers
Each Month (3 of whom actually pay the full price)

# COY-LINES   by Alison Wonderland

**What a jolly time of year this is!** Just that little extra cash to spend on the things we've always wanted. And so much to choose from! A drop of vinegar is just the thing for keeping your cistern free of sludge.

**All the ladies will know what I mean** when I say that they will be glad of a PAXTITE. No more awkward moments, for PAXTITE is thoroughly impregnated with lavender. Just drop me a line, and enclose 9d in stamps, I will send you a free leaflet, confidentially, under a plain cover, and addressed to your next-door neighbour.

**I do love a spot of prune juice,** but how it does affect one. Now NEWFOOD of Barnstaple have solved our housewives' dilemma with their new prune powder. Just sprinkle it on at any meal. Give your family prunes the safe way with NEW-FOOD Powder of Prune. (1/4 a tin or 4/- for three.)

**Most of us will be doing a bit** of bricklaying over Christmas. But you won't want nasty wet clinging cement all over your nice, clean, well-kept home. Your home deserves a SELWYN LLOYD PAINT SPRAY and MORTAR BINDER. No more filthy lino, no more weary dusting no more spotty floors, no more stubborn grime with an automatic, adhesive, rubberised Selwyn Lloyd Paint Spray and Mortar Binder. Just write to me, and I will send you a free sample.

**Your friends won't say anything**—you'll just see less and less of them. And more often than not, it'll be because of your ear odour. Play safe by getting some COLLINS EAR LOTION AND LOBE RESTORER today. And here's a tip—a recent survey showed that 98% of the British public had never heard of Collins, so get yours today before the rush. PS. And try it with fruit—it's delicious!

**I often feel like a piece of toffee.** That's why I'm so happy about Pulm's delicious new sweet treat, EVERLASTING STRIP. Just munch away happily for as long as you like, then pop it somewhere safe, and it's all ready for next time. And no wonder Everlasting Strip is so good—for it's Pulms who make Rollo-mints (the "too bad-to-swallow mints")!

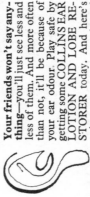

**Oh dear me, what shall I do?** How often we women say things like that, don't we? Well not any more—not with new all plastic NUDILON PANTILETS in the Duro-Masturbene Luxipaks (from Shermans the "Nudilon Pantilet People"). Fashioned in plastic, they are ideal for covering tables, giving a nice healthy tan, spraying dentures and using as imitation book shelves. So if there's something that makes you say "I've got a job that needs doing badly"—*Nudilon Pantilets!* Untouched by human hand—Shermans kick them into the packets. In three handy sizes: large, enormous, and where-can-we-sit.

**That's all for now.      I'm off to the shops again !      See you next month !!**

**Bye-bye for now !!!**

*Alison Wonderland*

---

## It Was First Class

### BY ELIZABETH MATTHEWS

*Twenty-six-year-old haulage contractor*

I FELT ALONE in the unknown. Here I was travelling across tracts of unfamiliar land in a dimly-lit train full of strange faces, peering and curious.

As the train set out for Gravesend, I felt that I had got to close a window. Every eye was on me. There was nowhere to look.

Then suddenly the young man sitting beside me turned and asked, "Don't you read the . . ?"

I nodded.

"I thought so," he said triumphantly.

"Why?" I asked expectantly.

"Well," he began slowly, "it was when you closed that window, I suppose. I remembered how they've found out about fresh air being one of the causes of cancer .. October 1962, I think, . . and how .."

"Yes, that's right," I said happily, "and now I look at you I can see you read the Digest, too."

"Oh," he said eagerly, "how?"

"By that hole in your shirt, of course."

"Ah, yes," he smiled, "my sweat-band modulator. Marvellous how Dr. Gromatov discovered that sweat runs in bands in our wonderful bodies, and that if we can .."

He stopped, placed his finger in the hole, and said sagely, "It's things like this that bosses are on the look-out for."

"I know," I said, "when I .."

So we went on. We talked all the way to Gravesend and passed through the barrier together. I was no longer alone. Nor was he. Thanks to the best traveller of all.

---

## Do Our Advertisements Help You?

*Yes, they do.* You see, when a manufacturer decides to market a fresh product—let's say a new tablet—he advertises.

You see his advertisement, and next time you are out you buy his tablets, because you know that the very fact that he advertises proves his goods must be *good*.

Thus our manufacturer sells more tablets and reduces his prices. And so it goes on. Soon everyone is better off.

And it's also the advertisements that help to keep Non-Reader's Digest the remarkably cheap magazine that it is.

*The*
VOLUME 83 Non-Reader's Digest ALL 1963

*The moving story of Millie Cooper, the Chicago woman, who became mother of the world's children*

# One Great Big INTERNATIONAL Happy Family

### BY MILLIE COOPER

MY marriage had crashed, my friends were dead, and my career was in ashes. I was deeply worried.

Then I decided I must not let life trample me underfoot, but that I must meet it squarely in the face.

So I offered to adopt a child. Imagine my surprise when three little Cambodian orphans arrived one morning. I was shocked at first, but then I realised that it was my duty to help them, and besides they would be a great help about the house. They were all girls, you see.

I soon learned their language and became very interested in Asia. The news began to get around, and I was offered a very well-paid job in a travel agency. Already I was feeling much happier.

I tried to share my good fortune with the children of the world by adopting another child. This time I wanted a boy. He turned out to be a bright-eyed little Somali, who had been uprooted from his homeland and brought to America.

Soon I became very interested in the social problems of Somaliland, and this in turn brought me further promotion.

Now I adopted four more of the world's kiddies. They were all different colours. One was black, one was yellow, one was white, and one was blue. He was so cold, poor little fellow.

When I went to the airport to collect them, I met a very handsome young pilot and invited him down to see my "miniature United Nations," as I used to delight in calling it.

He came, and soon we were married. Harry does not like children very much so we had to get rid of our little family, but not before they had all given me a present. My heart warms whenever I think of them. By deciding to adopt a child, I had found wealth, friendship, happiness, and Harry. I had received so much more than I had given. That, I suppose, is the real meaning of charity.

*Condensed from Christian Herald*

# Non-Reader's Digest Next Month

*The best advice I ever had*
by Lord Hailsham

*Twelve years to live*
The harrowing story of one man's fight against disease

*The friendly people*
A picture of the happy islanders of Samoa

*They flew for Frankie!*
The moving story of how two United States airmen flew 500 miles—for a five-year-old boy!

Plus Junior's got a gal! Your mind improves with age. It pays to pun, etc.

*Non-Reader's Digest does your reading for you*

### THE LAST WORD

A good dose of weedkiller will soon rid the house of aunts.
—CHIPPOLATI DAILY NEWS

The assembled company enjoyed some of Mrs. Benyon's delicious cat sandwiches.
—NEW YORK TIMES

Seem to have lost that zest for living? This article will help you to find it again

# How To Relax & Be Popular & Overwhelm People

From the case book of Dr. Herman Frock, the noted New York psychiatric consultant

MORE than 95 per cent of the neurotics who enter my consulting rooms are mentally ill. They are searching, and that is why they ask searching questions—questions that all of us are asking too.

How can I relax? How can I be popular? How can I overwhelm people?

The answer is to learn. Life is a school from which we must never quit. You must observe what I call "the rules that can conquer life".

To relax *consciously aim at a self that has sufficient.* Your peace can only come through plenty—the plenty of character, achievement, and possession. Try to reach the stage where you can look at your new car and say, "I have everything to be proud of". Or rather, "I have everything of which to be proud".

To be popular—*unceasingly consider the welfare of others.* Forget about yourself—think of your neighbour. Those were the words of The Greatest Psychiatrist Of All. Don't get wrapped up in yourself—make people convinced that they are your centre of interest.

To overwhelm people—*assert your personality.* Let those around you do as *you* want. Don't submit passively to their ideas and ideals. Mould them to your specifications.

These are my rules for life. Read them and follow them—you will never get better.

*Condensed from Happy and Healthy*

---

A Non-Reader's Digest Worst Person Award

# The Most UNFORGIVABLE Character I Have Ever Met

BY BOB SCHULZ

THE train moved slowly over the Rockies. My only companion was a tall man, with grey hair and ears that seemed to glow as we went through tunnels. Gradually my attention was drawn towards him.

"Nice train we've got here," I remarked.

"Life is like a railway engine," he replied.

"Yes," I said.

"Keep to the rails and you'll reach the everlasting junction," he rejoined.

By now my eyes were riveted on this strange and compelling figure. But he did not seem to mind.

"Who sleeps with a blind man, awakes cock-eyed," he mused.

I nodded thoughtfully. Was it really my good fortune to meet a man whose words were imbued with such wit and wisdom? I pinched myself to see if it was true. It was. I waited. Soon, as I had hoped, he spoke again.

"The ant is a busy insect," he reflected, "but he still has time to go on picnics."

"What?" I ejaculated.

"A woman is like a glove—you can put her on and take her off," he gibed.

"Ah," I chuckled.

"That's not true," he conceded.

"It's not," I breathed.

"No," he parried.

"Why?" I prompted.

"Because," he asserted.

"What?" I spluttered.

"Yes," he grunted.

"Oh," I muttered.

"The rumba is a means of waving goodbye without using the hands," he quipped.

"Yes," I voiced.

"Have you no more to say?" he enquired, gazing at me intently with those disconcertingly clear blue eyes.

"Well, I did wonder what made you think of the rumba," I mumbled.

"Dogs bark, but the caravan goes on," he chaffed.

"You mean," I started.

"The caterpillar is just an upholstered worm," he lampooned.

"Now I see where you're going," I suddenly disclosed.

"You see?" he demanded.

"I do," I nodded.

"Sure," he rumbled.

"Yes," I purred.

"Where?" he thundered.

"Well," I faltered.

"What?" he exploded.

I never saw him again. But I see now that I must never forgive him. I must never forgive him for he was unforgivable.

# What Teenagers Want to Know About Love Sex and Marriage

BY EILEEN VAUGHAN

*EILEEN VAUGHAN is a teacher who is also a mother. She is helping teenagers to understand their growing bodies. Miss Vaughan teaches a rather unusual kind of course at Gail River Secondary School, Illinois.*

WHILE taking this course I have often been surprised at the wide range of interests these youngsters have. But there are some questions which crop up every year.

I talk to the boys and girls in two separate rooms first, and then when they know most of the facts, I bring them together. Sometimes we get some quite surprising results.

*The boys ask:* Why do girls sometimes draw away when we want to kiss them?

I try to show them that there is a right way to kiss a girl, and a wrong way.

"Try it out on me," I smile, and persuade them to do just that in a frank and informal manner. Sometimes classes like this go on quite late.

*The girls ask:* Why is it our parents say one thing, and our boy friends another?

Before I answer this question, I always try to get a parent to come along and say what he (or she!) thinks.

"I never knew parents could be so intelligent," one student admitted afterwards.

Then I explain to them that boys of 17 and 18 are trying hard to channel their urges, sometimes unsuccessfully.

"Everyone's got a body," I remind them.

*Both boys and girls often ask:* Have married people got to have babies?

"No, they haven't," I assure them. I tell them that it is quite possible to be married and not have children, and that lots of people in our big cities are doing just that.

"But how?" they chorus.

"Well, of course, they could arrange it by living miles apart," I smile, and we all enjoy a happy chuckle at my silly banter.

"But that's not the best way," I go on seriously. Then I tell them about what science has done to help us. They are all very grateful.

The key to success in a job like mine is, I suppose, experience, and the principal often tells me that he has no complaints against me on that score. So I think it can be said that this new course is going down very well at Gail River, although I find that I have very little time to myself. There are so many people wanting to call on me.

Readers will be sorry to hear that Dr Herman Frock, the author of the article 'How to Relax, be Popular and Overwhelm People' on page 51 is at present suffering from the after-effects of a severe nervous breakdown, and is unable to see patients. We are sure you will want to join with us in sending Dr Frock our best wishes for his recovery, and a speedy return to his healing ministry.

♠

THIS MONTH'S COVER
*Robed priests in the Bernese Oberland sit down to a frugal meal. The priests wearing the colourful red scarves are elders, and are sworn to lives of complete poverty, chastity, and misery.*

---

*This is a book that had to be written—a book of and for the times in which we live. It is a book which proclaims that men's minds can never be made slaves to the powers of tyranny, in whatever part of the Communist world that tyranny be.*

# To Freedom

By Nicolas Shukin

*A special full length condensation*

IT was dusk in Omsk. I could hear the steel boots of the grim-faced guards as they paced up and down the stone corridor that ran parallel to my cell.

I was a prisoner. My family had fled to the South. They had meant to flee to the West, of course, but had lost their way.

I had realised I must be guilty, and confessed to the P.K.V.D. They were the Secret Police. They were so secret that I didn't even know what P.K.V.D. meant.

After my first confession, the guards used to bring me further piles to sign. These would often include all the unsolved crimes of Omsk.

After a few months suspicions began to crowd in upon me. Could I really have done all these things while I was locked up in prison? My faith in Communism was shaken.

I longed for freedom and managed to speak to one of the prisoners who had been to America. That was why he was in prison. He told me of the wide streets and careless people of the Free World.

Gradually a plan began to formulate in my mind. I decided to put it into operation. That night it was the turn of the youngest guard, Igor, to bring me my gruel. Gruel is all there is to eat in Russia.

Igor had just returned from the Korean War and as he passed the gruel through the partition, I whispered urgently.

"Free World."

Igor's expression did not change. He took no notice. He might for all the world have not heard anything. Unfortunately it turned out later that he hadn't heard anything.

I decided to try again. The next time he brought my gruel I said, loudly this time, "Free World."

I waited. A spasm of pain crossed his face and he was gone. Perhaps he had been eating too much gruel.

Would it be beating or the rope, I thought, as I tossed restlessly on the floor that night. There are no beds in Russia. Then I heard footsteps outside, I heard them turning the key in the lock—and the door was open!

I waited breathlessly, not daring to breathe, but then I heard a voice mutter "Free World", and I knew it was Igor.

. . .

We crossed Russia posing as Party Officers. We safely crossed the frontier. Soon we were in New York.

On the day we arrived, Igor and I walked up and down the teeming streets. I knew very little English, and even less American, but I was fascinated by the smiling faces of these free people.

Everywhere there were the signs and symbols of democracy, such as I had never seen before.

"Get your AUTOGRAPHED HAIRPINS now!"

"Holiday in MIAMI!"

"Defence Budget Doubled."

"A TV set for FIVE DOLLARS down."

I had found my Free World at last.

✒

An admirer asked Lionel Barrymore whether he liked love scenes on the stage. The great man drew himself up to his full height, and told her coldly,

"My dear Madam, I am perfectly aware that all the world loves a lover—until he starts to complicate the parking problem!"

✍

"A glutton is a man who takes the bit of pastry you wanted."

—ANONYMOUS

*"To Freedom" is published by the Goldwater Press at 15s.*

## 'HOW CAN I GET THE CASH TO PAY FOR MY WIFE?'

Caryl Brahms & Ned Sherrin

'My Boss is my rival for the hand of my girl. . . .'

WISE, *Nkaw Kaw.*

'My girl friend has just reported to me that she is expecting a baby and this embarrasses me. . . .'

KWESI J., *Accra.*

'I have a youngster aged eleven who is giving me a lot of trouble. . . . I haven't spared the rod and every time I give him a hiding he tells me that I'm wasting my time. . . .'

WORRIED MOTHER, *Benim*

'Since beating him does not help I would suggest you stop. . . .'

DOLLY

'I have two sisters and a male friend. Now this friend wants to befriend one of my sisters whereas both of my sisters want to befriend the same boy. . . .'

L. A. N., *Issele-uku.*

'. . . I am nineteen years old and in love with a boy of twenty-one. This boy placed me in the family way and then left town to go and work in another town. . . .'

THAN DIE, *Newcastle, S.A.*

'Tell me dear Dolly is this girl mad or what?'

AMOS, *Ibadan.*

Each one a cry from the heart and each cry firmly dealt with by Sister Dolly or Sister Priscilla in *Drum*, 'Africa's leading magazine'. Geography will decide which supplies the answer to the problem. Homey, cosy, schmoosy Dolly ('My dear young man, I will be the last person to discourage you in this affair since you and your girl seem to have taken on so nicely. . . .') or brisk Priscilla, straight from the shoulder ('Get rid of him kid, that's all.')

Dolly can be read in two editions of *Drum*, Ghana and Nigeria ('You can't go and divorce your husband just because he hasn't met your father.') Priscilla's sharp wisdom is on sale in South Africa only ('To heck with his nose-picking sisters. You just have faith in your man and hang on to him.')

Unlike their English sisters, Dolly and Priscilla are not dealing only, or even mainly, with middle-age dissatisfaction and teenage sex and its after-effects; indeed, the after-effects seem to offer no problem in Nigeria and Ghana ('I am in love with a woman of thirty-one. This woman has six children with a man she has been living with at her house. . . .' or 'So, Dolly, I would like you to tell me what I should do in order to marry the first girl in spite of the fact that the second one is now expecting a child from me?') Theirs is a

146

practical world of dowries and bride prices and lobola. 'How can I get cash to pay for my wife?' asks CHUKUS of Aba. 'I have thought of putting this girl in the family way and thus forcing her parents to let me marry her with or without dowry. But this has always been repellent to me as it looks terribly underhand. But what can I do to have this loving girl as a wife? I have no money; I can't go to a money-lender, and her parents won't let me have her on a sort of hire purchase. Dolly, have you any suggestion to make in the way of helping us along? I'll be jiggered if I don't marry this girl'.

Dolly can deal with this one.

'If you are an easterner, then let me remind you that the Government has enacted a law against high bride prices. . . .'

Priscilla ('Have you a love worry?'), even more a woman of the world, is crisper. S.M. of Pretoria had this problem:

'I am twenty-five years old and in love with a girl aged twenty-one' (most of the letter writers favour a direct approach). 'This girl has two babies with me, although one passed away. But this girl is giving me a headache. Of late when I call at her place she usually is not there. I only find the child, who usually tells me that she has gone out in a car with her former teacher. She usually comes back late at night and sometimes she sleeps out. I've tried to talk her out of this but she tells me that she is still a young girl and must do everything she likes.

'What should I do about this girl? Mind you, I've paid half the lobola to her parents but they don't say anything about what their daughter is doing.'

Priscilla's reply?

'Go to her parents and demand your money back . . . toss her overboard.'

In both Ghana and Nigeria in April and March of this year Dolly had to deal with a delicate problem. Both the lady and the gentleman seemed to prefer blondes—the negro equivalent of blondes that is. JANET from Akoko writes: 'Because I am more fair in colour than many Nigerians it has always been my ambition to marry a man whose colour is as light as mine.' But Dolly has no patience with these highfalutin ideas:

'When you really do fall in love, it will be difficult to check on his colour of skin.'

No more than she has with SUN-JACC of Kadima:

'Although I'm a married man, I have a weakness for fair skinned women. And the strange thing is that my wife, a very clever woman in many ways, does not know anything of it. . . .'

'You've got to get a grip on yourself or you'll find yourself in a pretty mess.'

When Dolly is not being severe, she has a quiet sense of fun. See how she deals with BOLA of Lagos:

'I am thirty years old, of average height, and hold a responsible post in the civil service. I want a literate wife who is between eighteen and twenty-five, light in complexion, of average height and moderately built. In short, a beautiful woman—preferably somebody whose first marriage has flopped due to the fault of her former husband. She should be a Yoruba by birth and resident in Lagos. Please help me, Dolly.'

'Here's a strange request, indeed,' says Dolly, but it doesn't throw her. 'Write to Bola c/o me, you beautiful Yoruba divorcees of Lagos, and I will forward your letters.'

Dolly takes in her stride another problem which would surely give Evelyn Home pause for thought:

'I am a sixteen-year-old boy in middle form three. Unfortunately I am rather tall and fat for my age and, what is worse, I have large breasts. . . .'

YAW ABBAN, Akimoda.

'In spite of the fact that I am a boy, I have large breasts which grow larger and larger as time goes by. . . . Kindly help me save myself from this odd state of affairs.'

WORRIED, Tamale.

'My advice,' writes Dolly, 'is see a doctor—fast!'

There is no doubt that Dolly's personality is very real to her readers. In December SAMMY, from Lagos, pays her court.

'Would you, on seeing this my photograph,' he writes, 'tell me of your immediate reaction after twenty-four hours. I have spent over £6. 6. 0 to gain your love by charms; my bush doctor took me to the town's cemetery where I buried the attached photograph for seven days and seven nights, and I am sure will charm your face whenever you look at it. Here are the words the doctor asked me to write at the back of the photograph: Dolly, I conjure you to love me by the name of Alpha and Omega (that old pair!), Tafawa Mumubu, Adona Kasubibi, Iyabe Shodikpo, Sunny Eleemeze. The more you look the less you see. Run away from your husband, if any, and make your way to Nigeria to look for me within twenty-four hours after seeing this my photograph. I command you again by Alfrodomo, Bundu, Kafacuchi Wadi, Alasaki Madi. Come, come, come—love is blind.'

However, love was not as blind as all that.

'Well, well, well! What a fool you've made of yourself, my dear Sammy! . . . I have received both your letter and photograph and haven't stopped laughing. What a silly way to waste six guineas!'

Dolly is constantly battling with the supernatural.

'My sister . . . went to the extent of going to "prophets" and "prophetesses" who told her that the boy I am in love with is not the right man for me.'

'Your sister is talking a lot of nonsense,' replies common-sense Dolly. 'Stick to your boy.'

There was nothing supernatural about the problem of KWESI J. of Accra. Now that his girl friend has had her baby he no longer wants to marry her. Kwesi J. is puzzled.

' . . . I find her attitude towards me has changed and that she now does not give me the sort of service she used to render me. . . . In my company she is very quiet and very much unlike her own chatty and playful self. All this is very strange and so I have a mind to sack her.'

The strange thing is that Dolly seems to think it necessary to find a reason for the poor girl's action.

'It is quite possible that her change of attitude stems from the fact that your attitude to her changed from the time she told you she was expecting a baby . . .' but she comes down firmly on the girl's side. ' . . . How can she go about smiling when her whole future has been made uncertain by the fact that you have deserted her?'

No matter how poor the correspondent he still finds Dolly understanding and inventive.

'I'm a child of poor parents,' writes EMAN, of Ibadan. 'My father and my mother, myself and my two brothers all sleep in one room. I'm now eighteen and am beginning to understand many things, but my parents have been letting me sleep just a few feet away from their bed . . . of late I have been finding it difficult to look mama and papa straight in the face every morning. . . .'

Dolly faces facts.

'It is their lowly circumstances that has brought this about. Why don't you get a neighbour of yours to put you up every night?'

Sometimes there is an uneasy suspicion that lonely-heart letters are written in the editorial offices; but just who, in just what office, could possibly have dreamt up this next one:

'I'm nineteen and an orphan—but not a poor orphan. My father, who died five years ago, left me and my sister some money and property. But since his death my uncle, who is supposed to be looking after us, has been doing himself fine on my father's money and property while leaving my sister and me to manage as best we can. Do you think it would be sinful of me if I found a way of getting rid of my uncle so that my sister and I may enjoy the good things our late father struggled to leave behind for us?'

SUNDRY, *Calabar.*

Dolly is quite clear on where she should take her stand. 'I have never approved of those who do others in, no matter however justifiable their grounds for doing so.'

Write now to Dolly for advice:
P.M. Bag 2128, Lagos, Nigeria,
or Box 1197, Accra, Ghana.

or if you want a short answer—try Priscilla.

## CONGRESS FOR CULTURAL FREEDOM    Kenneth Tynan

AND NOW, a hot flash from the Cold War in Culture. This diagram is the Soviet cultural block. Every dot on the map represents a strategic cultural emplacement—theatre bases, centres of film production, companies of dancers churning out intercontinental balletic missiles, publishing houses issuing vast editions of the classics to millions of enslaved readers. However you look at it, a massive cultural build-up is going on. But what about us in the West? Do we have effective strike-back capacity in the event of an all-out cultural war? What is our answer to the Red threat?

Well, part of it is an organisation called the Congress for Cultural Freedom, founded in West Berlin in 1950 for the defence of our cultural liberty. Supported by American money, the Congress has set up a number of advanced bases in Europe and elsewhere, to act as spearheads of cultural retaliation. These bases are disguised as magazines and bear code-names—the English one, for instance, is known as *Encounter*, which is short for 'Encounterforce Strategy'. A spokesman of the Congress for Cultural Freedom told me something about its long-term aims.

'Our aim at Congress H.Q. is to beat the Reds in the culture race, and to that specific end we've launched a crash programme to achieve what we call "cultural over-kill". Let's spell that out in terms of the map. Here in Britain, as you've said, we have *Encounter*, which is a soft, undefended base. We also have three hard satellites—*Soviet Survey*, *The China Quarterly* and *Science and Freedom Bulletin*. Then we've sponsored *Preuves* in Paris, *Der Monat* in free Berlin and *Tempo Presente* in Italy. We think of that whole cluster as a kind of cultural NATO. Way up here in Sweden there's *Kulturkontakt*—and *Perspektiv* in Denmark completes the chain to the Federal Republic, and down to Vienna, where we have *Forum*. Over in India we have *Quest*, which is strictly non-militant and merely carries out highbrow flights to gather information about cultural weather conditions. And right here in Tokyo we have *Freedom-Jiyu*. We also have magazines in Mexico, South America and Australia—but the main pattern is what you see on the map. Cultural containment, or, as some of the boys like to put it, a ring around the pinkoes. In fact, I wouldn't say we had an aim. I'd say we had a historic mission. World readership.'

Q: Would you say there was a cultural gap between us and the Russians?

A: Well, that depends what you mean by culture. Take poetry, for example. It's true we've had trouble getting our poets off the ground—there are still a lot of bugs to be ironed out, and I guess we could all name a few of them. As of now, the Reds have greater fuel-power when it comes to getting poets off the launching-pad—a guy like Yevtushenko can outsell Betjeman and Frost many times over. But against that, you have to remember that one of the reasons they buy a lot of poetry is that they don't live in a free economy where they could spend their money on genuine consumer goods.

Q: How about the culture gap in the theatre?

A: Same difference. People in the Eastern block have to live on a steady diet of serious theatre, subsidised by public money. They aren't allowed to see things like 'Goodnight, Mrs Puffin'. That's what I mean by slavery.

Q: How do you feel about censorship?

A: Anti—absolutely anti. But of course it's a powerful factor in the Russians' cultural push. You see, they can compel their artists to turn out easy trash, like propaganda slogans, instead of difficult trash, like TV commercials, that have to prove themselves in terms of hard cash.

Q: And the Congress came into existence to combat this state of affairs?

A: Exactly—to remind the Russians that Western culture is still the ultimate deterrent. And we won't give it up unless they agree to dismantle theirs.

Q: How do you feel about phased disarmament? Suppose they promised to suppress a Polish film magazine, would you give up *Encounter*?

A: Well, we want deeds, not words. Where cultural supremacy is concerned, you can't trust the Russians.

Q: How would you define cultural freedom?

A: Freedom to be anything but Communist. We have no quarrel with Communist writers, merely with what they write.

Q: Do you screen contributors to your magazines?

A: Hell, we're not McCarthyites. We don't exclude anyone. If a guy's a security risk, we get him to write on non-political subjects.

Q: In an all-out cultural war, what sort of casualties would you expect?

A: Hard to say. They'd take out Broadway, of course, and most of the West End theatre, but on the whole I think we'd survive—although an awful lot of free cultural tripe would be wiped out in the process. But whatever happens, we in the Congress feel it our duty to keep our bases on a round-the-clock, red-warning alert—always watching what the other fellow is doing, instead of wasting valuable time on scrutinising ourselves. Basically, what we oppose in the Soviet bloc is the fact that the people who pay the piper are philistines with no special knowledge of the arts. People like the Minister of Culture and so forth.

Q: And who finances the Congress for Cultural Freedom?

A: Well, among others, the Miami District Fund, Cincinnati; the Hoblitzelle Foundation, Texas; and the Swiss Committee for Aid to Hungarian Patriots.

Q: Do you think both sides should concede the right to inspect cultural sites?

A: Well, *we* grant *them* reasonable inspection rights, although God knows there isn't all that much to inspect.

Q: And should we allow them to export their cultural bases to foreign soil?

A: That's an iffy one. Ballet—yes, never harmed anyone. But as for openly aggressive, first-strike theatrical emplacements like the Berliner Ensemble in East Berlin—there I draw the line, and I have to say an emphatic freedom-loving no. We don't want their so-called 'technicians' swarming around on our very doorsteps.

Q: So you think we were right to forbid the Berliner Ensemble to come to London in the spring?

A: Yes, on that matter I think I have to go along with the State Department—I mean the Foreign Office. Or rather, I don't *think* I have to. I *have* to.

## ONE READER WRITES    Keith Waterhouse & Willis Hall

ON THE 25th September, a certain citizen was moved to communicate the following intelligence to the letters column of the *Daily Express*:

'An Air Force husband is definitely the best there is.' Signed, *Mrs B. J. Burtenshaw, Hughenden Road, High Wycombe, Bucks.*

Earlier in the week, Mr F. C. Herbert of Wembley, Middlesex, contributed this historical fragment to the letters column of the *Evening News*.

'I thought you might be interested in these details on a bill I paid in 1912. Four foot six inch bedstead, one pound four and sixpence. Wire spring, thirteen and sixpence. Wool mattress, fifteen and sixpence. Bolster, four and sixpence. Two feather pillows, thirteen and sixpence.'

Message ends. . . . Why do people write letters to newspapers? Who writes letters to newspapers? What is the home life of *Pro Bono Publico* really like?

*Mr Hargreaves, a city clerk, sits down at a table and begins to write on a pad. Mrs Hargreaves enters and places a vase of flowers on the table. She tries to glance at what her husband is writing but he secretively shields the writing-pad with his arm. Mrs Hargreaves sits at the table opposite. There is a moment's silence.*

MR H: How do you spell 'perambulating'?

MRS H: One 'm'.

*Mr H. makes an alteration in his letter and seals it in an envelope with a flourish. There is another silence.*

MRS H: What have you put?

MR H: How do you mean, what have I put?

MRS H: What have you written?

MR H: You'll see it, when it's in print.

MRS H: I always have to wait.

*Mr Hargreaves, with a long suffering sigh, tears open the envelope and reads out the letter.*

MR H: Dear Sir, Coming home from work this evening I saw four or five kiddies perambulating up and down the street, singing Christmas carols. Do you not agree that with sixty-three shopping days still to Christmas this is, to say the least, a bit much. Yours, etc. No Scrooge.

*Another silence.*

MRS H: They won't publish that.

MR H: Of course they'll publish it. (*He broods for a moment*) Guy Fawkes in July—I got that published. Peter Piper's Pungent Post, *Daily Sketch*. Sixteen/six/sixty-two. (*Brooding again*) Why do pop-singers get more than nurses—they published that.

MRS H: You never told me about any carol-singers.

MR H: I didn't think you'd be interested.

MRS H: You don't like telling me things.

MR H: Twaddle. I often wish you'd listen to the many interesting things that happen to me as I go to and fro.

MRS H: We never hold a conversation.

MR H: Well . . . (*Striving to please her he racks his brains for something interesting, and finally comes up with*): Seen on Albert Bridge today. A frog merrily hopping towards Battersea.

MRS H: (*Impressed and mollified*) You didn't.

MR H: (*Striving to top himself*) Seen in Cambridge Circus yesterday. A policeman munching a hamburger. What a spectacle for foreign tourists.

MRS H: You see, I'd have been interested to hear that.

MR H: (*Proudly*) I hold many opinions as well. (*He searches his mind for an opinion*) I realise the programme planners of BBC and ITA are not wizards, but why, oh why, does 'Route 66' clash with 'Z-cars', thus ruining our Wednesday evening viewing?

*Mrs H is now spurred to join in.*

MRS H: Indeed. And why oh why do we have to be left 'up in the air' at the end of so many plays, thus ruining our Sunday evening viewing also. Have playwrights forgotten how to tie up the loose ends?

*Mr Hargreaves is excited at having got a response from his wife and as she speaks is impatiently stabbing his finger, waiting to produce yet another opinion. He starts almost before she has finished.*

MR H. Why do garment manufacturers never consider that those of us with perhaps a more rotund figure would like a look-in at the exciting new trends in men's wear?

MRS H: In this age of space miracles and rockets, when is some down-to-earth genius going to present us with a sauce bottle that does not clog?

MR H: I regularly travel first-class on a second-class ticket and will continue to do so as a protest against Dr Beeching's inflated salary.

*The flow of conversation has warmed them to each other, and they smile fondly.*

MRS H: Seen in my local High Street. A busy stream of flowing traffic held up while a mongrel dog of dubious ancestry sauntered leisurely over the zebra crossing.

MR H: (*Genially shaking his head*) It never did. (*He considers for a moment, then his expression changes*) All dogs should be destroyed in the interests of public hygiene. And I speak as an animal lover.

MRS H: Who says that cage-birds are colour-blind? My neighbour's budgie, Peter, can recognise blue and yellow. It can also say 'Swinging' and 'Dodgy'.

*There is a pause, for they have run out of things to say. Mr Hargreaves remembers something.*

MR H: I have in my possession a copy of the *News of the World* dated August, nineteen-nought-two. Dress shirts are three shillings each.

MRS H: I still have in use a bread-knife purchased by my grand-mother.

*There is complete unity between Mr and Mrs Hargreaves and again they smile at each other fondly. Mr Hargreaves takes up his writing pad and begins to write, dictating as he does.*

MR H: Dear Sir, In an age of television addicts and hi-fi are we the only couple in these benighted islands who still indulge in the old-fashioned art of conversation?

# Come Home Sunday Pic!

## As told to Keith Waterhouse & Willis Hall

**Folk said I was heartless because I tried to sell my baby to the *Sunday Mirror*. They do not know the true facts, they do not understand that behind this seemingly selfish front lies a young mother's anguish.**

It is true that I attempted to barter my baby's future in Fleet Street pubs, but is there a mother in the land whose heart does not cry out in sympathy?

A few short weeks ago we were a happy family—my hubby, my kiddies and the *Sunday Pictorial*. We are not rich and you can surely imagine the simple delight with which we would sit down to the *Pic* after a good Sunday dinner.

Guilty Doctors, Unfrocked Parsons, Homosexual Headmasters, Murderers Who Paid With Their Lives For One Small Slip!

All these we loved and cherished as part of our way of life. How long ago now it seems to those happy days when I was reading about Witchcraft in the Midlands and the Religious Sect that was nothing more than a Cloak for Sin. And then, overnight, something happened to my dear old *Pic*. I blame the satirical television programmes with which it has been associating, although there may be other causes.

At any rate, the *Pic* changed from the happy, family rag we loved into the new, swinging, way-out, way-ahead, get-with-it, satirical *Sunday Mirror* of today. I do not understand what has happened.

In vain I have appealed to the *Sunday Pic* with which I have spent so many happy years to return. I will do anything to bring it back.

I have promised it a signed confession of Sodomy In A Preparatory School and of Midnight Orgies In The Mansion Home of A Leading Cheshire Industrialist.

**I have offered it a full exposé of the editor of the** *People* **who lords it in a council flat while his staff live in hutments and caravans.**

I have created single-handed a shocking traffic in Shetland ponies, but all to no avail.

Now, a desperate mother, I make this final appeal to the old *Sunday Pic*. Come home now and I will sell you my son, Kevin, aged five, for fifty pounds.

**I will authorise any series you like on the subject of Guilty Mothers.**

As I make this dramatic appeal, my children are peering out of the window, looking in vain for the *Sunday Pic*, which I dare not tell them will never come. They are not old enough to understand why it has changed its sex and become another *Reynold's News*.

**With tears in my eyes I say to the *Pic*: Come Home—My Babies Need You.**

AM. Read the papers — smoke a cigarette. No news to speak of, no jokes to draw. Outside, sun shining on rooftop, birds singing. Inside, cigarettes and a litter of papers. "All part of growing up in big city" says family man Birdsall. Striped shirt, shaggy haircut denote 'young angry' intellectualism.

1·00 p.m. Ideas taking shape. "Seed of idea sown first in subconscious, later seeps into conscious expression" quips humorist. Coffee-cup empty, sun still shining. Soon drawing will begin in earnest. Calm before storm, most difficult time. (Note steely eye-glint)

m. Cartoon "swinging along easy" says long-haired jokester. Trying time still to come, when drawing submitted to editors. "Half artist, half salesman" is Birdsall's realistic self-appraisal. No more coffee. Time to start drinking. "After 3 doubles laughs come easily" sums up cartoonist.

5·00 p.m. Five cartoons rejected, one hour to deadline. Rejects already accepted by rival publication, hard work over. Now comes easy bit. Drawing of Mr. Kruschev chasing Adenauer. "High-ups will think up caption, bless'em" says scribbler-prophet. End.

# 11 Postscript

*Re-THE BEDSITTING ROOM*  The Lord Chamberlain

*Endorsement of Licence No. 3133 dated 31st January 1963*

THIS LICENCE IS issued on the understanding that the following alterations are made to the script:

ACT I

*Page 1*  Omit the name of the Prime Minister: no representation of his voice is allowed.

*Page 16*  Omit '... clockwork Virgin Mary made in Hong Kong, whistles the twist'. Omit reference to the Royal Family, the Christmas message and the Duke's shooting. Substitute wording as details in Mr Miles' letter of 14th January 1963.

*Page 21*  The Daz Song: Omit 'You get all the dirt off the tail of your shirt'. Substitute 'You get all the dirt off the front of your shirt'.

ACT II

*Page 3*  No representation of Lord Home's voice is allowed.

*Page 2–8*  The mock priest must not wear a crucifix on his snorkel. It must be immediately made clear that the book the priest handles is not the Bible.

*Page 2–8a*  Omit 'the good book'.

*Page 24*  Omit 'crap' substitute 'Jazz'.

*Page 2–10*  Omit from 'We've just consummated our marriage ...' to and inclusive of '... a steaming hot summer's night'.

*Page 2–13* Omit from 'In return they are willing ...' to and inclusive of '... The Duke of Edinburgh is a wow with Greek dishes ...'. Substitute 'Hark ye! Hark ye! The Day of Judgment is at hand'.

ACT III

*Page 3–7*  Omit 'Piss off ... piss off ... piss off ...'. Substitute 'shut your steaming gob'.

*Page 3–12/13*  Omit the song 'Plastic Mac Man' and substitute: 'Oh you dirty young devil, how dare you presume to wetting the bed when the po's in the room. I'll wallop your bum with a dirty great broom. When I get up in the morning.'

*Page 3–14*  Omit '... the perversions of the rubber ...'. Substitute '... the kreurpels and blinges of the rubber'. Omit the chamber pot under bed.

## CLOSE DOWN Keith Waterhouse & Willis Hall

*A suburban couple sit staring at the television set. Although programmes have finished for the night, it is still switched on.*

M: It's over then.

R: Yes. It's all finished.

M: It won't be on next week.

R: No. It'll be something different next week.

M: I thought it was good.

R: (*Judiciously*) On the whole. On the whole.

M: Well, it was something different.

R: Well, it was satire, wasn't it? What *we* call satire.

M: All jokes and skits and that.

R: Yes! Mucky jokes. Obscenity—it's all the go nowadays. By law, you see. You're allowed to do it. You can say bum, you can say po, you can say anything.

M: You dirty devil!

R: Well, he said it! The thin one! He said bum one night. I heard him! Satire!

M: It's a wonder they weren't all put in prison.

R: No! Far from it! It's encouraged! Then you have what you call *double entendre*. There, like I might be sitting here talking to you, and I say something and you take it one way but it's got another meaning. It's got a mucky connotation. You can take it which way you like. (*Thinking of an example*) Like, 'Take your knickers off'.

M: They never said that!

R: Not in as many words, no. I've forgotten how they said it but it was the general gist of it. *Double entendre*—it's all the rage. For example, I might be sitting here, you might be sitting there, and I might say, well, I might say anything. But what it really means to an agile mind is, take your knickers off.

M: How?

R: Well, it does, it just means that. It's generally recognised. It has a satirical context.

M: They want locking up. It's a good job they are coming off.

R: There you are! You've got it! You've cracked a *double entendre*!

M: How have I?

R: What you just said. You said, it's a good job they're coming off—meaning, them on the programme. The persons. But I could take it two ways, you see. What it could mean is, take your knickers off.

M: But you don't wear knickers.

R: I don't, but you do! You see, if I'd said it—what it could mean to a dirty mind is: Take—off—your—knickers.

M: I haven't got a dirty mind. (*Giggles*) They're not coming on again till September. . . .

R: Very good. Excellent. I shall quote that.

M: (*After silence and with delicacy*) Bum.

R: Po.

M: I liked him that did the drawings.

R: Very good band, too. What they call far out.

M: Anyway, it's finished.

R: Yes, it won't be on next week.

M: Shall I switch it over?

R: Go on then. (*With relish*) We might get the last ten minutes of 'Whiplash'.

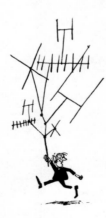

# Credits

BY NO MEANS everything in TWTWTW is scripted. This book represents a choice made from the best of the material submitted to the show as well as many items that have been specially written or designed. Writers' credits appear with their contributions.

All the drawings in the book are by Timothy Birdsall and Trog with these exceptions: *Annabel* (pp. 42–43), *But My Dear* (pp. 50–51), *Attlee* (pp. 98–99) and *Hullo Fans* (p. 138) by William Rushton; *Wilson* (pp. 87–89) and *Mother's Day* (p. 91) by Barry Fantoni.

All the photographs in the book are by Lewis Morley with these exceptions: pages 26–27, 58, and 73 by John Timbers; pages 33 and 52 by Keystone Press; pages 33, 52, and 117 by Camera Press.

Faces in the photographs included: p. 10 Roy Kinnear; p. 13 Barbara Windsor; p. 18 Michael Redgrave; p. 19 Fenella Fielding; p. 43 Sybil Thorndike; p. 90 Rose Hill; p. 92 Kenneth Cope; p. 100 Lance Percival; p. 118 Al Mancini; p. 128 David Kernan; p. 132 David Frost; p. 155 Timothy Birdsall.

*Filth* on pages 24–25 and *Attlee* on pages 98–99 were written by David Nathan and Dennis Potter. The drawings on pages 49 and 134 are reproduced by kind permission of the *Spectator*.

We would like to add our thanks not only to those who have contributed directly to this book, but also to those who have done so indirectly—by their television contribution:

| | |
|---|---|
| *Assistant Producers* | JOHN BASSETT |
| | PETER CHAFER |
| | JOHN DUNCAN |
| | ALISON EYLES |
| *Designer* | MALCOLM MIDDLETON |
| *Musical Director* | DAVE LEE |

And the final credit, of course, is the BBC's, without whom neither book nor programme would ever have seen the light of day.

*Mr. Fearson,*

## *To John Larney, Shoemaker*

| 1799 | | s | d |
|---|---|---|---|
| Nov. 16 | Clogged up Miss | | 10 |
| Dec. 14 | Mended up Miss | | 2 |
| | Carried up | 1 | 0 |
| 1800 | Brought up | 1 | 0 |
| Jan. 3 | Toe-tapped master | | 3 |
| April 1 | Turned up, clogged up, and mended maid | 1 | 6 |
| May 1 | Lined, bound, and put a piece on Madam | 4 | 6 |
| May 10 | Soleing the maid | | 8 |
| 14 | Tapping Madam | | 6 |
| 15 | Putting a piece on Madam | | 3 |
| 16 | Stretching and easing little master | | 3 |
| | | 8 | 11 |

*Settled,*

*John Larney.*